FINDING
A JOB THAT
LOVES YOU
BACK

CARLY INKPEN, JUSTIN WRIGHT, AND TAD MAYER

FINDING A JOB THAT LOVES YOU BACK

THE **THREE CONVERSATIONS**
THAT WILL TAKE YOU FROM WHEREVER YOU ARE
TO WHEREVER YOU DISCOVER YOU WANT TO GO

HABITUS
INCORPORATED

Finding a Job That Loves You Back:
The Three Conversations That Will Take You
from Wherever You Are to Wherever You Discover You Want to Go
Copyright © 2023 by Carly Inkpen, Justin Wright, and Tad Mayer
Habitus Incorporated
Boston, MA

For reprint permission, write to publishing@habitusincorporated.com.

To contact the authors for interviews or to invite them to speak,
visit habitusincorporated.com/finding-a-job-that-loves-you-back.

Discounts for bulk purchases by nonprofits, schools, corporations, or other
organizations may be available. Write to publishing@habitusincorporated.com
to inquire.

Cover design: Neela Samia

Library of Congress Control Number: 2022914997
ISBN, print: 978-1-7379469-0-8
ISBN, ebook: 978-1-7379469-1-5

Printed in the United States of America
27 26 25 24 23   1 2 3 4 5 6 7 8 9 10

Certified

Habitus Incorporated is a

Corporation

Contents

PHASE 1

Finding Clarity:
Conversations with Yourself

PHASE 4

Building Greater Fulfillment: All Three Conversations

You Are Here

Finding a job is one of those things that most of us feel like we should know how to do at a certain point—like cooking. It can seem like everyone else knows how, or that no one really does except an exceptionally confident, supernaturally focused few. That or it's the exclusive realm of the privileged, well connected, or smarmy. But here's what the three of us know from our own experience, as different from one another as we are: Finding a job is something you can learn to do, learn to be good at, and even enjoy.

Like cooking—or photography or whatever skill you take pleasure in—learning how to find a job that loves you back requires getting a handle on some basics and then practicing until you reach a point where you're happy with the results, and with the process itself. And like beginning to develop any skill, looking for a job can feel impossibly vast, opaque, and awkward when you're starting to learn, and on top of that, it often feels intimidating. Unlike cooking now that food delivery apps are so convenient, it's unavoidable for almost everyone. But finding a job that really works for you—that you find fulfilling and that serves all of your core needs—has such huge fundamental benefits for your life that learning how to do it is absolutely worth the effort.

This book is for you if you know you need to change something about your career but you're not sure what exactly to do next. It's for you if you've never looked for a job before. And it's for you even if in the back of your mind the idea of a job that "loves you back" seems unreasonable. It isn't. <u>You're competent and sincere, and you want to love your job.</u> <u>You *deserve* a job that gives you as much as you give it</u>—a job that loves you back.

Maybe you're just starting out and you have a job you love already—the work, the people, the industry, or mission—but it's a small company and there isn't much room for you to grow and advance, or the pay is too low for the long term. Or maybe you're five or ten years in, your job pays well, and you're about to be promoted into the role you thought would be ideal and went to school to get. But that job is going to require sixty hours a week, a lot of stress, minimal appreciation, and a lot of corporate political nonsense, and you just can't see yourself continuing in this direction much longer. Either way, now what?

It can be hard to see anything but very limited options. Whether you had an excellent career center in college or grad school, or studied for a specific field or trade, or didn't have access to any guidance at all, it's very common to feel unsure of yourself, stuck, and constrained.

We've been there. We've coached a lot of people who've been there, and we've learned, adapted, and developed a lot of realistic, effective ways to determine the first step that comes after being stuck, and then the next and the next, until a promising—often unforeseen—path begins to open before you.

That's why we know that these skills and approaches are useful at any stage of any career. In this book, though, we focus primarily on people who are fairly early in their careers, from people who feel like they haven't landed their first "real" career job yet to people who are established but feeling the need to make some kind of change. College and graduate students who want to think concretely about what to do after they graduate will get a ton out of it too.

Once you've read this book, we're sure you're going to keep it handy so you can read it again—this part or that part, when certain sections become especially relevant again at various points throughout your career. That could be when you need a new challenge, or you have a life event on the horizon, or an unanticipated opportunity comes up and you need to decide what to do—keep the great job you have or take the leap to something new.

The three conversations we will be walking you through—that have served us and our clients and colleagues so well—will help you in all of those scenarios, and in many others. That's because they always start from where you are. They help you find not only clarity about what's most important to you and what direction to start in, but also people who will happily help you on your path in many more ways than you can imagine.

As the three conversations become familiar to you, and then comfortable, you'll start to look forward to them. Feeling confident about your next step—and curious about where the ones after that will lead you—will make progressing in your career seem less like rowing solo across an ocean and more like a road trip with friends. You'll also become better able to help other people in your expanding community to find jobs that love them back too.

No matter where you are right now, whether you know where you want to go but not how to get there, or aren't sure what direction you want to try, this book will get you to your next step and beyond.

—Carly, Justin, and Tad

Getting There

When you're planning a road trip, the first thing you do is choose your ultimate destination. Then you plan your route there, and maybe a different route back, so you get to go even more places. Maybe you'll visit friends or family somewhere along the way. But how do you decide where to go and how to get there?

The destination might seem obvious at first. You've wanted to see the Grand Canyon since you learned about it in middle school, or you wanted to experience Montreal because your aunt has told you stories about when she lived there in her twenties. The route—or at least parts of it—might seem mostly obvious at first. Of course, you'll take the main highway. It's what everyone does. Las Vegas is near the Grand Canyon, so you'll definitely stop by. Or wait, should you skip Las Vegas and try to make it out to the Pacific Coast instead?

Less obvious are all the influences behind your road trip decisions. Why did the Grand Canyon or Montreal capture your imagination in the first place? Some of those influences are easy to call to mind. And then there are the reasons behind those, plus the conscious and unconscious practicalities you factored in when you were deciding among numerous possible destinations and routes.

The decision-making that goes into looking for a job isn't all that different. The big difference is the stakes. For a road trip, the stakes are low—it's all about discovery, adventure, getting away, and enjoying yourself—you can go anywhere and it'll be great because you're on vacation! A job search can feel much more overwhelming at first. Once you've finished this book, though, what might feel like a high-stakes chore will become an approachable project. You'll also start with a focus on discovery, and that will open up a wider range of career choices than you realized you had.

This book will help you learn how to find jobs that will love you back—at this point in your career, and throughout, because you'll get better and better at it. A job that loves you back meets all of your most important needs and requirements for your work life. Yes, all. Appropriate compensation is almost always on that list. Some of the other categories include culture, environment, schedule, variety, and a sense of accomplishment. You'll learn to get much more specific about your priorities, and that will allow you to identify a wider range of possible jobs rather than a narrower one.

We know this because it's what we've learned ourselves—first independently, and then, through conversations among the three of us. There's more on our story a little later. For now, just know that it's completely okay if you feel like you have almost no idea what you're doing when it comes to finding *any* job, much less one that will love you back. There's no secret formula, there are no unsavory "techniques." Sincerity and the willingness to practice something in order to become good at it is all you need to get started.

An Investment in Yourself

Reading a book is a time commitment, and we take that seriously. This is an investment you're making in yourself, and you'll be glad you did. It takes practice to make something new become natural, and the time, focus, and effort you allocate to this investment in yourself will be worth it.

Some of you are reading this book at the very beginning of your careers. Fantastic! You'll use and benefit from what you learn throughout your working life. Most of you are in your first or second or third job, and there's a reason you're looking for a change.

You could be looking for a change for a lot of reasons, like frustration because your work feels invisible, or there are no advancement opportunities, or your workplace culture is toxic. It could be boredom because your work has become routine and no longer challenging. It could certainly be that you're just not paid enough for a comfortable life, including saving for the future, especially considering all the effort you put into your job. The reasons we look for change are often negative, it's true, and that's okay. The next time you decide it's time to look for something else, the aim is for it to be for a more positive reason: you need a new challenge, or you want to move to a small town or a redeveloping city, or you've thought of a new way to apply what you're good at in order to make a big difference in your community. Each skill you learn here, and each step you take, will make it easier for you to make that next change.

We've been working on this book for a long time, and during that time, the global pandemic has caused a lot of people to reevaluate their work lives, and a lot of companies and organizations to reevaluate whether they're good places to work, and the way they hire and retain people, including both employees and contractors. A lot of good can come out of all of this reflection. By no means is everything going to get better for everyone automatically, especially considering the inequality and exploitation people can face in the working world. Your investment in learning how to find a job that loves you back will reinforce the positive trends that are starting to take root during this period of workplace reevaluation.

Whatever your reasons are for looking for a new job—and there are always multiple reasons—you're in good company, and there's a lot of good to be gained here—for yourself and others.

The Origins of the Three Conversations

At the most fundamental level, finding a job that loves you back comes down to having conversations. By becoming more and more intentional about your career-related conversations, you will get more out of each one as a result. The three conversations you will have are with yourself (about what's most important to you), with connectors (people who can give you insight and introductions), and with decision makers (people who can give you work). It was even conversations that caused us to realize this.

Just before we met in 2011, each of us was independently struggling in our own way to break into the field of conflict management, or, as it's sometimes called, alternative dispute resolution. Professionals in this field help others resolve disputes, as well as teach negotiation and conflict management skills to individuals and organizations. As aspiring practitioners, we were knee-deep in collaborative negotiation theory—a powerful approach to managing differences and coming up with mutually beneficial agreements. We were learning to be mediators, and we were captivated by the way people could find common ground and resolve even seemingly irreconcilable conflicts. But work in this field was hard to come by.

Established firms and practitioners wouldn't trust us with any substantial work until we had experience, but there were precious few ways for beginners to gain experience. Paid work for people junior in the field was almost unheard of, and even unpaid opportunities were scarce. And yet, despite rocky starts and some demoralizing dead ends, each of us found ourselves advancing more quickly than expected.

Before we met, we had found creative ways to access mentoring and training opportunities. We collaborated with established practitioners to create internships, part-time jobs, full-time jobs, and freelance projects that otherwise wouldn't have existed. We formed partnerships and built community. And then we found ourselves involved in fascinating projects, like running a conflict resolution workshop in the cloud forests of rural Mexico, training soon-to-be diplomats in mediation techniques, and running a team-building retreat for a Spanish multinational pharmaceutical company.

All the while, we continued to immerse ourselves in the current thinking and practice on negotiation and conflict resolution. We attended lectures, audited courses, and later worked as teaching assistants in continuing education courses. All of this training prepared us to teach negotiation skills to businesses and non-profits, and eventually teach our own courses on negotiation and behavior change at top universities.

We eventually came to realize that *what* we were doing—negotiation, mediation, collaboration, and communication—had also become *how* we were developing our careers: The tools of our trade—our negotiation and communication skills—were also enormously useful for sourcing work opportunities.

After we met, and while we were getting to know one another in conversations at work, we found ourselves comparing notes on how we'd gotten there. The more we talked, the more patterns began to emerge: There were certain skills that seemed to benefit everyone, broad stages that many people experienced during their working lives, and certain mindsets and attitudes that fostered career advancement and fulfillment. What was working for Justin was also working for Carly and Tad, even with our notable differences in personality and background. Everything hinged on the way we had been having conversations with other people along the way.

It turns out that for as much as finding a job is something *you* need to do, finding a job that loves you back is actually a collaborative project. And that means conversations, or collaborative negotiations.

Since we come from the collaborative negotiation field, the word "negotiation" is one we use all the time, so of course we're comfortable with it. For a lot of people, though, it can have stressful, adversarial connotations: Salary negotiations. International hostilities. Hostage situations. But what we're talking about with the term "negotiations" is collaboration, and includes everything from negotiating for a new job to the way you decide what to do for dinner. It means taking into consideration the needs, and wants of everybody involved and coming up with a plan that meets everyone's needs well enough, whether that's you and your partner deciding what to cook or a group of colleagues deciding who will take which responsibilities on a team project. In terms of career development, it means that everyone involved has things to offer and considerations to make in an effort to accomplish something together. Conversations focused on collaboration are the way to figure out what's to everyone's benefit.

If your primary associations with negotiation are the stressful ones, it might take a little time to shake those off. We completely understand, and we've written the book with that in mind. Fortunately, the conversations you'll be having at the beginning—your first collaborative negotiations—are with someone who's familiar to you: yourself. Not only will they be more fascinating than you're expecting, turning up many useful new insights, but they'll also really help your perspective shift from the anxiety of feeling stuck to the confidence of having a sense of direction and clarity on what you're looking for and where to find it.

How We Know

We've organized the patterns we noticed in our conversations together—many, many conversations over ten years or so—into four phases involving the three conversations.

Phase 1: Finding Clarity focuses on your conversation with yourself, helping you to get clarity about what matters most to you and defining that it would actually look like to have a job that loves you back. In Phase 2: Increasing Access you will figure out, mostly through conversations with connectors, what the primary needs and barriers to entry are for the field you want to enter and how to become a desirable candidate for the opportunities you want. In Phase 3: Getting Work You Love, equipped with your knowledge of your desired outcome, and having become an attractive candidate, you will have conversations with decision makers to get a job you love. Then, in Phase 4: Building Greater Fulfillment, you'll take a step back to assess your new level of satisfaction and consider what adjustments to make in order to achieve a work and personal life that is fulfilling for you.

We each stumbled on this insight by virtue of simultaneously breaking into a new industry while also learning collaborative negotiation skills. The direct application of these skills became obvious when we met and started comparing notes.

After we recognized how effective this approach was, we experimented with it more intentionally and organized it according to the four phases. Our own earlier career development experiences, though, definitely did not feel organized at the time. The three of us are very different people, and some of us did feel more of a sense of direction than others. But this is one of the reasons why we know that the approach to finding a job that we describe in this book will really make a difference for you.

To demonstrate this, we're sharing the twists and turns of our own paths. This has the added significant benefit of previewing for you the way the three conversations work. We've included short first-person sections as illustrations of what we're talking about throughout the book as well, along with some fictionalized vignettes to add to the variety. Most of these were inspired by coaching clients we have worked with.

Our three stories will resonate differently with you, which is exactly the point. The fact that the three conversations we'll help you practice came from such different personalities and trajectories shows that you will be able to apply them well too. You'll see that a destination isn't always in sight, but that each conversation and each "next step" reveals your path.

Carly's Story

I went to a nondescript state school with no particular reputation. The academics were strong, I had a full-ride scholarship, and I found my way into thrilling extracurriculars that took me to study abroad in France, teach HIV-prevention in India, and work with female fish farmers in Bangladesh. I majored in the most practical of subjects, English literature, with minors in ecology and international studies.

By graduation I'd learned a lot about postmodern poetry, critical thinking, aquaculture, international development, and how to speak French with embarrassing grammar. But in a sea of thirty thousand other students, I never met anyone who knew how to translate these skills and arcane interests into a career. There were no learn-to-network seminars or fancy internships, no peppy career advisers or wise mentors to help me think about my future. I'd probably heard the phrase "It's not what you know, it's who you know," but it certainly didn't sink in. That sounded like advice for Ivy League hotshots and social-climbing business majors, not for an introvert like me. I graduated haplessly into the 2008 recession and followed my then-partner to Boston, a city where I knew no one and had no idea how to find a "real" job.

After endlessly spamming résumés into the void in search of an administrative assistant role, I got desperate and started going door-to-door. I spotted a Help Wanted sign that led to a minimum-wage job in a soul-crushing corporate café. I felt lucky to have a job, but it wasn't how I'd pictured using my honors degree.

Working at the café, I overheard a customer talking about his job resolving environmental disputes related to fish farming. This piqued my interest, and I asked him about his work. He explained that he was a mediator and facilitator in the field of conflict resolution. I'd never heard of that, but after some googling I asked him for an internship and was "hired" at the conflict resolution consultancy as an unpaid intern to refurbish their website. I fit the internship around a part-time paying job, but the only reason I could take this internship was because I had no student debt and I had the privilege of financial help from my parents for the first year after I graduated.

That internship—which did eventually turn into a paid administrative job—was my first glimmer that, perhaps, connecting with other people was the way to make headway in my career. I realized, after connecting with this customer, that I'd been oblivious to the community that was already around me. We don't always realize what's in our proximity. It was a springboard into an entirely different way of thinking about the working world.

I met Justin when we were interns at the conflict resolution consultancy together. He was the first person I'd run across who was comfortable consistently asking for others' advice and guidance as part of building his career. Following the advice he got before graduation, he intentionally asked people about their career paths, and sought advice about his career dilemmas. When a respected negotiation trainer had a seminar coming up, Justin offered to show up the day before to help her print and bind the course materials. This was helpful to her, and it gave Justin an invaluable hour to pick her brain; she later hired him to be a teaching assistant. When everyone in Justin's network said he just *had* to seek advice from Moshe, a top mediator, despite being a little intimidated by Moshe's status, he reached out. Moshe was willing to meet, but between family and grueling work travel, he had no time. Justin ended up traveling to and from Moshe's son's basketball practice with him and talking en route—kicking off a collegial relationship that continues today.

These moments of relationship building cost Justin only his time, but they were things I never would have thought to do. In my early days of job hunting, Justin connected me to an affordable mediation training course. He also asked the instructors of the negotiation seminar if he and I could be co–teaching assistants together, splitting the pay. The instructors okayed it since it didn't cost them more. Justin opened up valuable opportunities for me, but even more, he and I were learning together that job hunting and negotiation are not what we had assumed—being fake and schmoozing with people in fancy suits. Advancing in your career and negotiation are about talking to people. The more genuine and open the conversations, the more likely they are to be useful. The more people you talk to, the more you're able to get connected to a community of supportive, like-minded people—even for an introvert like me. Justin and I were realizing that we could use the very same negotiation theory we were learning at work to collaborate with mentors to invent creative opportunities for our career growth.

I enjoyed mediation more than being a cashier at the café, but I wasn't hugely passionate about it. Cobbling together various part-time jobs, I was barely making enough money to survive. I was looking for something more fulfilling—something that would allow me to have a positive impact on the world and give me a comfortable lifestyle. But I had no idea what would be fulfilling for me, and I spent several years feeling very lost.

My first forays into mediation made it clear that working with people was one of my driving interests. But, mediation just didn't quite fit. Over the next couple of years, I realized that I wasn't satisfied finding practical solutions to immediate conflicts. I wanted to get to know my clients better, to dig deeper into the roots of their conflicts and understand how they navigated the world. But what job would let me do this? Eventually I started going to therapy and it dawned on me that *this* was a job that might allow me to meet my various interests. But how did one become a therapist? Could I afford to do a long graduate degree? Would I be able to make a good living? I had a new project ahead: figure out what it was actually like to be a therapist and how to get there. Luckily, Justin and I had learned how to tackle this kind of project.

I knew it couldn't be tackled online. I needed answers from real people. At first, I had no idea who to talk to. However, I read something about the New York Psychoanalytic Institute and wondered if there was one in Boston. Turns out there is, and they offer free lectures open to the public. Perfect, a room full of therapists; surely I could manage to talk to one. After a particularly interesting lecture, I emailed one of the presenters to ask if she'd be open to meeting for an informational interview. She generously told me all about the various possible graduate school options and explained her day-to-day life and the pros and cons of her work. She connected me to some other therapists, who then put me in touch with others. She also suggested that I apply for an entry-level mental health job at a nearby hospital, which I did. I thought I'd be too inexperienced to get hired, but psychiatric hospitals see their fair share of conflict, and they were impressed with my mediation experience. Slogging out to the suburbs to work the 3 to 11 p.m. shift on a substance abuse unit, I added Mental Health Worker to my list of part-time jobs.

This yearlong process of informational interviews and learning the ropes in a challenging entry-level job confirmed that becoming a therapist was the right path. Yet, the process of going from administrative assistant/mediator/mental health worker to psychotherapist still seemed pretty vague and overwhelming. Luckily, the people I'd met in my informational interviews helped lay out the concrete steps I'd need to get there: apply to social work school, make sure I got good supervision during my graduate internships, identify any desired areas of specialty, and find a postgraduate fellowship for advanced training.

Graduating from social work school, I was a very different person than the English major who graduated cluelessly into the 2008 recession. It has become second-nature to use my negotiation and communication skills to identify my career needs and interests, and weave a professional web of colleagues who share similar goals.

Social work is emotional work, and you need a strong support network to withstand the inevitable blows that are the cost of doing this business. I feel lucky to have colleagues who have become friends, who are deeply supportive, who will listen when I need to vent, who will help me think through thorny clinical problems, and who are as improbably passionate about combining psychoanalytic theory and social justice as I am. But, peel away the luck, and there was a series of considered decisions that helped seed the ground for these rich, nurturing professional connections to grow. As I got to know the field of social work, my negotiation skills allowed me to find job openings that could meet my particular needs as well as niche communities of people within the profession who share my motivations.

As always, there are things I wish I'd known going into social work, hazards that my informational interviews didn't uncover. I wish I'd understood before starting out just how broken and unjust the medical system is in the US. How this contributes to mental health work being undervalued and underpaid. How infuriating it is when I see an insurance company or Child Protective Services fail one of my clients. It was clear from my informational interviews that plenty of mid-career therapists make a comfortable living. But I hadn't anticipated that in my first year out of school I'd make less than $30,000 working full-time with no benefits in one of the most expensive cities in the US. Or that I'd have to supplement my income by participating as a guinea pig in paid medical studies for six months until I found a second job.

It wasn't until I'd been in the field for a while that I realized just how significant the income difference is for a therapist working in community mental health versus a therapist who has their own private practice. Negotiating with myself about my lifestyle interests and needs, I decided that I'd start a part-time private practice. It's no small matter, starting one's own business, but I knew a network of people who'd already started their own practices and who could answer all my questions. And I had a community of people who would lament with me over drinks about how much it sucks to be complicit in a classist system where the high cost of therapy makes mental health care inaccessible to so many people. *And* I have a community of colleagues who are activists and writers, working to change the ways the mental health system harms people.

I've learned that finding a job that loves me back is about many things, like making a comfortable living and being in a role that never feels repetitive, where I can continually learn and grow. Above all, the most important factor in making my work life enjoyable and sustainable was understanding my own needs and interests well enough to find a strong network and a good community of like-minded peers, colleagues, and friends who had similar needs and interests.

Justin's Story

I was twenty-four years old and nine months out of college when I moved to Boston to start my career. I was older than most of my peers, having repeated sixth grade because, despite being a native English speaker, my reading and writing skills were subpar, thanks to studying in Spanish from the ages of four to nine in Nicaragua. I

chose Boston because it is one of the intellectual hubs of the negotiation and conflict resolution worlds. My plan was to spend five
years learning everything I could about the subject and then jump
into the nonprofit or activist world that felt more like home to me
and where I hoped I could put the skills I would learn in Boston to
use, creating social change.

I come by my overly ambitious save-the-world energy honestly.
I grew up in a family committed to social justice. My parents, moved
by the destructive US intervention in Nicaragua during the Reagan
era, founded a sister city project connecting our hometown of New
Haven, Connecticut, with Léon, Nicaragua. We all moved to Léon
as a family when I was four. This experience gave me an appreciation of the deep unfairness of the US approach to capitalism and
foreign policy. I studied political philosophy, economics, and ethics
at an Ivy League university to try to better understand how free-
market capitalism, which sounded so good on paper, ended up producing such unjust and horrible outcomes for so many people at
home and abroad.

My early attempts to find work in the field of negotiation and
conflict resolution ended in utter failure. This was in no small part
due to arrogance and naivete: I thought I could skip the conventional job application process and just show up at each business in
turn, ask for a job, and be given one. I went to every company I
could get a meeting with and said some version of, "I so admire
what you do. I want to learn about negotiation and conflict resolution. I'll do whatever you need—get coffee, make photocopies, or
even cut your lawn. Please just give me a job that will allow me to
learn." Not surprisingly, that strategy resulted in a lot of rejections
and no jobs. Meanwhile, I was also applying for EMT jobs but not
making great progress on that front either. Discouraged, I started
looking for job postings in the negotiation and alternative dispute
resolution space but was rejected or received only radio silence.

Fortunately, some timely advice from a good friend led me to
a new approach. He suggested I talk to as many people as I could
about the work world and get their advice *before* trying to get a job.

Trusting my friend completely and not knowing what else to do, I started asking people who worked in the negotiation and conflict resolution field for informational interviews. Some people generously volunteered their time to tell me their stories and give me advice. Others were too busy or simply had no good reason to meet with me. Through my conversations and the rejections, I learned three things. First, if I wanted to get someone to talk to me, much less give me a job, there had to be something in it for them. Second, no one was willing to take the risk of hiring people entering this field without experience. Third, the things that senior practitioners in the field seemed to need most were well-organized logistical support, note-taking, and teaching assistants to do course coordination.

With this information in hand, I changed my approach, now trying to figure out what the specific people in the field I was interacting with cared about and how I could meet those needs. I had a few lucky breaks early on where I got opportunities without having thought deeply about what the other person or organization cared about, like the internship where I met Carly at an organization focused on complex large-scale facilitation. But in most cases, when I did not think about the other people's needs, I was not able to get the meetings or the opportunities I wanted.

Next, I negotiated with a top-notch Boston-based mediation company to intern for them in return for getting to take all of the negotiation and mediation courses they offered for free. I was able to stay on at the facilitation organization as a contractor, helping to do research and support important non-urgent projects for brilliant facilitators who had time to mentor me because I was around on a regular basis doing work for them. I did a research project for a negotiation and mediation clinical program at a local university in exchange for getting to take an amazing weeklong executive negotiation program that I could not afford. I was lucky enough to get to run my first negotiation training course under the guidance and mentorship of Tad. I knew from my informational interviews that if someone like Tad, who worked at the mediation company at the time, took the risk of letting me co-train with him, I had to show up strong or I would not get another chance. I practiced my parts of the training alone, with pets and friends, until I was confident I could impress Tad with how well I knew the content and could run the parts of the course he had delegated to me. Sure enough, all my preparation paid off and Tad generously allowed me to join him for more training in the future.

By the end of my first year of working my way into the negotiation and conflict resolution field, I had done scores of informational interviews, volunteered on dozens of trainings, and mediated over eighty cases as a volunteer mediator in district court. I was learning a ton but barely scraping by. The only paid work I could get was note-taking, course coordination, and logistical support work. I survived by sleeping on friends' couches before splitting a two-bedroom apartment with two other friends, eating mainly peanut butter sandwiches, and generally keeping my expenses low in every way I could manage. But I wasn't able to fully cover the bills and was burning through my savings.

One of the people I scheduled a conversation with shared that the money was in corporate training. The idea of corporate training did not appeal to me, but being able to cover my expenses really did. So I started asking for people's advice on how to get corporate training gigs. One of my mentors pointed me to an organization that ran trainings in Spanish. Since I am a fluent Spanish speaker, I managed to get work with them, first as a course coordinator, and eventually as a trainer. From there I managed to get onto the trainer rosters for several of the negotiation training companies in the area, which gave me consistent work and a more sustainable level of income.

After four years in the field, a colleague and I decided to start a business together, which we named Habitus. We began by servicing other training companies, but over time we started getting our own clients. We went after what no one else wanted because we still relied so heavily on the mentorship and work opportunities other companies in our space provided. We did not want to be seen as a threat or competitor. So, we ended up taking projects like a six-week negotiation seminar in Shanghai, China. For me, it was an amazing experience, but for most of my colleagues, who had kids and families, that amount of time away was a deal breaker.

Our business continued to grow, but I kept feeling the pull of social justice work and environmental sustainability. So once again, I sought advice. Through a few conversations, I discovered the world of mission-driven business and Certified B Corporations. My business partner and I immediately set out to certify Habitus as a B Corp and started to build relationships with the B Corp community, which felt like going back to square one. I had built trust and a solid reputation in the negotiation and mediation field, but no one in the B Corp world had ever heard of me or Habitus. But this time, I knew how to use collaborative negotiation skills to build relationships and find mutually beneficial ways to create work.

Over the next several years, I found ways to build relationships that met the needs of the people I wanted to work with, while deepening my connections to the B Corp community. I volunteered on marketing campaigns to raise brand awareness for B Corps and worked with a collective of B Corps taking action around climate change. As of this writing, Habitus has a growing team of trainers and facilitators doing a mix of the corporate work that pays the bills and the mission-driven work that drew me into this field in the first place.

Tad's Story

As a career coach, I thrive on deep one-on-one interactions that help clients find those aha! moments. If you had told me when I was coming out of college, though, that a professional role involving important conversations would fulfill my passion, I never would have believed you.

I attended well-known schools and got a strong education. In college I learned to act as an extrovert even though I was an introvert. Before I graduated, I had a couple of short stints as a stagehand for a ballet company.

When I went home to Long Island and told my father I was going to move to Utah and join the union to become a theater floor electrician, his response was clear and succinct "No." So with the help of a close college friend who had already landed a job, I took my communication studies major and joined a global advertising agency as an assistant media planner. This led to a couple of other large company gigs—in yield management and pricing for an airline and in partner marketing for a hotel chain. With each move, I became more unhappy in my career.

With some help, which is detailed later in the book, I pinpointed what was important to me, and it was as far from big corporate as it could be. Even with my earlier pursuits, I had had no idea. It was quite a moment for me when I realized that following the jobs that I thought I *should* pursue didn't fit with any of my priorities. That's what led me to shift to conflict resolution and eventually career coaching.

It was the conversations with people I knew, was introduced to, and reached out to along the way that created opportunities for me. For example, to move from the airline to the hotel chain, I contacted the head of the hotel chain's yield management and pricing and told him I was interested in learning more about their company as a place to work. I said that I would be really interested in discussing the differences in airline and hotel yield management and pricing, and even be happy to share some best practices. He quickly accepted the conversation, which helped me understand a lot more about the inner workings of the hotel chain and put me in touch with an opportunity there.

When I wanted to shift to small companies and conflict resolution, though, I had no idea where to start. So I accepted an invitation to a local alumni networking event hosted by my alma mater focused on marketing, since I was in partner marketing at the time. Someone stood up to introduce herself to the group and said, "I used to be in marketing and I am now a mediator. If you have any workplace or client disputes at your company, come see me because I can help." I raced over to talk with her because I had identified being a mediator as a target role for me since it was about the most prevalent opportunity in conflict resolution.

That conversation opened the world of mediation-related training, trade organizations, and companies to me. Later, after I had procrastinated about signing up for a mediation training, she even called me a week before it started and asked me if I'd registered yet. When I said no, she asked me why not. I had no good answer, so I signed up right after our conversation. She really went to bat for me.

Out of one connection, I was able to create a group of collaborators in conflict resolution who educated me on the ins and outs, and then I built a career. I landed a job at a leading negotiation and conflict resolution firm in Boston by offering to help with marketing if I could expand my role in mediation with the company.

My opportunity to pivot to career coaching came when Justin asked if I wanted to join him and Carly on this book project ten years ago. I was in the process of leaving my job so that I could focus as exclusively as possible on being a practitioner. Justin asked me about what was important to me, and that conversation brought back to the front of my mind what first motivated me to want to become a career coach. I had been through two major job searches and wanted to share what I had learned with others.

That conversation also helped me realize that coaching skills overlapped broadly with being a mediator. Considering (a) my clarity about how I could help job seekers, (b) the skills I had developed as a mediator that I could transfer to being a career coach, and (c) the opportunity to create an innovative approach to job searching, I was in!

And it just so happened that years earlier, my work with an industrial psychologist had resulted in four options: mediation, arbitration, training, and writing a book. I had already realized that arbitration was not for me (it's more about telling people what to do, versus helping them come up with their own agreement). And I had indeed become a mediator and a trainer. Writing a book was the last one on the list! That conversation with Justin opened the door to fulfilling that goal. While writing the book and starting my career consulting firm, I completed coaching training.

As I got my private career coaching practice off the ground, a colleague suggested that I learn about outplacement, which is an important part of the field that I knew nothing about. Outplacement firms are hired by companies to offer career consulting services to people whom the company has recently laid off.

To help me learn about outplacement, my colleague connected me to his former outplacement consultant, a vice president at a top firm in the Boston area. Let's call her Jasmine. She was (and still is!) about the most dynamic and energetic person I had ever met, and was more passionate about career coaching than I could have imagined. She also exuded curiosity about other people (me, in this case). We hit it off right away. I asked her about her career and why she chose to pivot to career consulting from another field (an overlap in our stories). She then gave me an overview of how outplacement worked. I asked questions, and then Jasmine shifted the conversation to something of interest to her—how my mediation and coaching skills overlapped.

After the informational interview, I sent a thank-you email and kept in touch with Jasmine by forwarding resources that I thought would be of interest to her and sharing her posts on Linked-In. Although my goal had been to learn about outplacement and build a relationship with a colleague in career consulting, Jasmine thought of me when an opportunity came up at her company, which I landed.

I could never have arrived at my current job, one that loves me back, if it weren't for the help of so many people along the way. Each of those relationships started with a conversation. Some people helped me figure out what was important to me in a next job, others shared information about target roles, and still others connected me to opportunities. If it weren't for those conversations, my clarity would not have been as sharp, my access to opportunities as strong, and my knowledge going into interviews so thorough.

The Next Steps on Your Own Path

As you can see in our stories, we all started out in different places, took different paths, and found very different but equally satisfying work. Reading them, you probably thought of your own story to this point, and maybe you've already started to feel a new sense of possibility. You may have noticed also that our stories followed the arc of the three conversations.

The idea of fulfillment will come up throughout the book. It's basically shorthand for a work situation that both meets your needs and makes you happy. We aren't pitching vaguely defined "dream careers" or writing with the assumption that everyone wants to start their own company and retire and then start more companies. Fulfillment will look different for everyone, and the path there—the next step, the first job that actually loves you back, and then the next one—is ongoing as our lives change and our ideas of what fulfillment is for each of us changes with them.

The rest of the book is organized to follow the four phases. In each one, you will focus on a discrete goal. Phase 1: Get clear on what you want. Phase 2: Get access to the kind of work you want. Phase 3: Get a job you love. Phase 4: Get clear on what fulfillment looks like to you so you can adjust your life. Within each section we will dedicate a chapter to how each of the three conversations—with yourself, with connectors, and with decision makers—support that phase. In each phase there is one conversation that will be of primary importance but the other two can provide complementary insight along the way.

Each chapter contains advice and process steps, while several contain exercises you can do alone or with a friend or colleague. Four of the five exercises in the book fall in the first phase because in order to follow any of the advice in this book, you first have to learn a fundamental skill—identifying your underlying needs, aspirations, and desires. Much of the first phase is focused on this skill applied to yourself—figuring out what matters to you. But this same skill will be vital for your conversations with connectors in Phase 2 and of utmost importance in your conversations with decision makers in Phase 3.

If you haven't already, you're about to start feeling a sense of possibility. You've already taken an important step: deciding to dedicate some of your time to learning a new skill that will serve you well for the rest of your life.

And you're about to dive into the four exercises that are in Phase 1. Take a quick glance through the short worksheets that go with them to get a sense of the space you'll want to give yourself when you decide to do the exercises. You'll definitely want to actually do them, too. You might decide to read all the way through chapter 1 first, and that would be a perfectly good thing to do. You can do each exploratory exercise after that, when you can dedicate the time and focus you need for each one.

Always keep in mind that the exercises are all about helping you find *your own* path to a job that loves you back. They're meant to be enjoyed! If you start to struggle with a question, leave it for a while and come back to it later. You're learning a whole new skill, so it's only natural that some days the ideas and insights will come to you more easily than others.

You can print out the PDF versions of the worksheets or use your device for the digital versions. Draw scribbles and arrows or drag and drop—or both. Whatever works best for you.

And keep going. With time and practice, you will get better and better at something that affects all aspects of your life—your work. Even before you come to enjoy the process, you will find that you're far more relaxed in it, and that alone will be a huge accomplishment for a lot of people. You'll feel this happening throughout Phases 1 and 2, and you'll experience it even more when you get to Phase 3. Phase 4, is probably further out in the future for a lot of people, but even if it feels that way to you, what it will give you in its brief form is a view of where the path you're on could lead.

In the meantime, as you read the whole book, make notes on places to return to. A lot of you will probably read through Phase 1 (chapters 1–3), do a quick pass through the exercises as you come to them, and then when you finish chapter 3, schedule the time you need to immerse yourself in each exercise. An approach along those lines will allow you to internalize the ideas and let your mind start the shift from feeling stuck to sensing direction.

By giving yourself the time and headspace for reading, working on the exercises, and practicing, you'll gain more and more confidence in your ability to decide what to do next, adjust your course based on your new insights and experiences, and identify many more possibilities than you can think of right now. You've started on a journey of discovery and new destinations.

Finding Clarity

Conversations with YOURSELF

YOUR
INTEREST
PROFILE

INSTRUCTIONS: Pages 54–56

Your Interest Profile is an ever-evolving list of your specific interests. Frame interests in positive, future-focused terms. Prioritize your list by putting a star next to the four to six that are most important to you.

LIST OF INTERESTS

1

Discovering What
You Want the Most

Now that you're here, you're officially in Phase 1 of your job finding project! This part is all about getting clarity on your most important personal motivations—the ones that are driving what you want in a job. By learning how to identify and describe these—to yourself and others—you'll be able to identify a set of possible careers that could fulfill your needs well. It might not sound like it, but this is a big undertaking. Fortunately, it will also be eye-opening and energizing.

Most of the established professionals we've interviewed or coached over the course of our own careers had significant misadventures and some outright failures before they found fulfilling work. We certainly did in our careers, as you saw from our stories. Over and over we hear people say, "When I graduated into the professional world, I had no idea what I wanted to do" or, "I thought I wanted to do X and then found out it was totally not for me, and I had no idea where to go next" or, "Utter failure left me lost and confused until I sat back, really thought about it, and then did something else." Interestingly, not many people mention their experience of lostness unless we explicitly ask them about it, or ask them to reflect back on their work history. It's as if, after emerging from a period of haziness and confusion, they charged ahead and unintentionally perpetuated the myth that successful professionals start out clear, confident, and directed.

In the workshops we've taught and with the people we've coached, we've seen people fall into the same two traps: (1) limiting their focus to what they already know and (2) casting too wide a net without clear criteria for evaluating all their options and then ending up overwhelmed by the sheer volume of what they find.

You limit your focus too much when you look for another job a lot like the one you've got now, just incrementally better somehow. It's what you know how to do, you've got experience and maybe education that directly applies, and it's the track you're on—where you have the best chance. But a variation-on-a-theme job might not be that much better or might be better in some ways and worse in others. These kind of similar but different opportunities can be hard to jump to because going to something like what you are doing now can feel hard to justify given all of the costs associated with switching roles coupled with the risk of the unknown.

Casting too wide a net without criteria for selection can look like this. You decide you want to do something totally different from what you do now. You come up with three or four exciting ideas, but you don't really know enough about any of them to make a choice. You're sure you'd love each of the fields you're considering, but your education and experience won't tell that story to anyone who's hiring for jobs like that. To make matters worse, two of the fields you're excited about have significant up-front costs to be able to enter —time and money for training and credentialing. It seems risky to sink years of your life and a lot of money into something you aren't sure will be a good fit for you.

The cause of both of these mistakes is skipping over the question "why" to the question "what." Rather than asking, "What is the job I should go to next?" your first step should be to ask, "Why do I want a new job?" or put differently, "What is important to me?" The question "What job should I go to next?" is a good question—people just ask it too early. Once you are clear on why you want what you want, then you will be able to move to the questions of where and how to get it. But it really is possible to get to a much better place in your work life. Reassuringly, as personal productivity expert David Allen argues in his book *Getting Things Done*, the key to getting unstuck is figuring out the next step.* Just the next step and not the whole plan. Getting clarity on your most important motivations is the first step toward being able to completely circumvent that deflating sense of being stuck. Getting clear about what's most important to you will help you evaluate the very-similar-but-not-totally-the-same-job situation.

When you know and can articulate what matters to you most, you will have a much easier time asking the right questions of people who work at the potential new organization to figure out if your needs will be met there. Having clarity about your needs and motivations also helps solve the too-many-directions problem. It will help you get advice from connectors in the various fields you're considering about which one would best give you what you're looking for. By having this first conversation with yourself to determine what you want, you'll find that clarity—and start to feel less stuck.

Lots of people don't just feel stuck, though. They feel lost, too. This is also completely normal, especially at the beginning of something or when looking to make a change. A sense of "lostness" is especially common in this particular context because discerning a career path and searching for a job are skills that very few people feel like they have. Uncertainty accompanies any attempt we make to redefine our path in life, but it's still usually hard to embrace being lost as a necessary part of self-advancement. Few of us receive direct advice, let alone counseling, about how to navigate periods of lostness as we mature in the world. The consistent theme from the many people who have graced us with their stories is this: being lost well is about figuring out what you care about before you try to figure out how to get it.

Phase 1 of finding a job that truly benefits you, that gives you fulfillment, is about making the transition from feeling lost to having a clear, thoughtful, and tested direction.

---

* David Allen, *Getting Things Done: The Art of Stress-Free Productivity*, rev. ed. (New York: Penguin, 2015), ebook chapter 1.

A Whole New Thought Process

At first, "discovering what you want" might sound too obvious. Certainly, everyone contemplating a change can list things they know they want. Identifying them in a way that helps you figure out how to act on them, though, involves a completely new thought process for most people. You'll probably be surprised by how much effort it takes to put your deeper, most meaningful motivations into words that feel right to you. We know it will be worth it, though, and that you'll find it not just interesting but enjoyable once you've had some practice at it.

This chapter offers three exercises to get you thinking broadly and productively about the activities and experiences you find most compelling or meaningful. They're designed to help you look beyond the assumptions you may have about what kind of jobs would be a good fit for you. Beneath your assumptions that you work best on teams or that you want more responsibility are deeper needs that a job on a team or with more responsibility would meet. The most important purpose of the set of exercises in this chapter is to help you make a dramatic shift in the way your mind works when you're thinking about your career—to establish a habit of identifying and naming your deeper motivations.

Three of the five exercises in the book are in the first chapter because making this shift takes some time as well as effort. And learning how to reach past the usual thinking that leads to feeling stuck and lost is essential for establishing this new thought process. Each exercise teaches a different path to the same kinds of insights into what is important to you as you make choices about your career. Your work on the exercises will culminate in what we call an Interest Profile—a foundational document you may very well find yourself referring to and modifying for years to come. The document isn't long or complicated. But the awareness it represents and the clarity it reflects will guide and give confidence to every step you take on the way to a fulfilling career.

The term "interest" comes from our background in teaching collaborative negotiation. Rather than meaning something you're curious about or that you enjoy—such as being interested in butterfly migration or following Formula 1 racing—it refers to your needs and wants. If you're a bit uncomfortable with this meaning at the moment, that's probably because for a lot of people it appears to mean just "self-interest" and to imply someone putting theirs ahead of someone else's. We definitely don't mean that. Interests do address things like salary and benefits, yes. But they also include things like the kind of life you want to lead and the impact you want your work to have.

Interests are the foundation of *collaborative* negotiation, which is all about working together for the best outcomes for everyone involved. For people to figure out together what the best outcomes are, they need to know what everyone's needs and wants are, and in negotiation lingo, those are interests. They're the underlying needs, desires, and goals that inform what we want—the reasons why we want those things. And negotiation is the process of talking those things through—a conversation.

Our aim with this chapter, indeed with this whole book, is to show you how to direct your job search with intention and become more confident in your career development, and to do that, you need to know and be able to articulate your interests. It's through conversations you'll have, first with yourself, that you will reveal your interest in full depth. Discovering your interests will then reveal possibilities—avenues that just weren't visible at all before.

Shifting to Focus on Interests

When you feel stuck, uncertain about your next step, or even completely lost, it's easy to imagine that there's a single perfect solution lurking just out of sight. The problem is that real life rarely works like that. Focusing on a single "right answer" often obscures a wider range of possible paths—any number of which might lead to a good, fulfilling outcome.

In the collaborative negotiation field, we refer to these mythical perfect solutions as "positions." They're your requirements, and there's nothing wrong with having them. "I want to be a patent attorney." "I want to own a BMW." "I'm going to become an electrician."

Everybody wants certain things, especially when it comes to job searching. The unnecessary limitation occurs when you don't know how to look beyond your positions and articulate for yourself *why* you want those things. Everybody has a whole host of complex reasons why they want what they want.

Why do you want to be a patent attorney? "Because I want to be respected." Why do you want to own a BMW? "Because then I'll know I'm successful enough that I'm not worrying about money." Why do you want to become an electrician? "Because I like working with my hands and I like the variation in the job—constantly solving different problems and meeting different people."

If you focus on a position, there is only one way to achieve your goal. If you step back and look at the interests behind the position, many avenues for achieving that same goal open up. There are many ways to build a good reputation and demonstrate financial security. There are plenty of jobs that offer lots of variation and allow you to work with your hands.

To illustrate how positions—rather than a deep understanding of needs—limits people, consider Laura's situation.

Laura recently left her job as a bank manager after doing it without much satisfaction for several years. The hours were fixed, the commute was long, and she had to deal with chronic staff problems. But she stuck with the job so long to support her partner, a social worker by training, who worked the last few years on minimal pay to found a nonprofit that serves people experiencing homelessness. She knew she needed a change—for her sake and for her partner's—but also didn't have a clear transition in mind. Soon after her partner's nonprofit reached a stable footing, Laura's bank unexpectedly downsized and needed to lay off one manager, Laura volunteered. After her last day, she was both relieved and deeply concerned about what her next move would be.

Faced with this kind of uncertainty, many people retreat and look for a similar, familiar job, even though there's a high likelihood of it ending up in the same dissatisfaction. Laura, though, knew deep down that she had to make a significant change, and that it had to come quickly. She leapt at a new idea, one that seemed to be staring her right in the face: yoga instructor. Over lunch, one of her friends suggested that she become an instructor at Om, a nearby studio that the two had been going to for years. Laura loved the idea. Something just felt right—no more commute, no more staff issues, no more paperwork. But more importantly, she had been training for this in her spare time for years and had always been told by her instructors that she was a natural. This was it.

But when it turned out that there were no jobs at Om or at any other studio in the area, Laura was utterly deflated. She couldn't go back to her old job, and the one she had gotten really excited about simply wasn't available. So what to do?

This kind of career limbo happens a lot because people often jump from the reasonable idea of making a career change to immediately focusing on one specific job option. That one option represents a position. On the surface, this thought process is completely logical: if you want a new job, you decide on what that job should be and start applying.

Obviously, at some point, the vast majority of us will have to hunt for a (singular, specific) job. But while this hunt is a necessary step in joining, rejoining, or transitioning in the workforce, it's not the first step. You stand a much better chance of getting to a place where you are doing work you love if you first take the time to gain clarity about your interests and think about the different ways those interests can be realized.

In order to find fulfilling work, you first have to figure out what you're seeking to accomplish through your career move and to articulate that in a compelling way—to yourself, first and foremost. Knowing the interests that are driving you toward a certain type of work and make you enthusiastic about your work life may not seem to point to a specific job, but they will nonetheless guide your job hunt. With some effort, they will eventually point to many exciting job options.

Underlying Laura's desire for a specific position are interests—the needs, goals, fears, and desires that motivate her to pursue that position. In Laura's case, her position is:

- Be a yoga instructor

But perhaps her interests are:

- Focusing on her own work instead of management or administration
- Greater fulfillment from every day—spending less time commuting
- Integrating health and wellness into her work life
- Having a schedule flexible enough to be a present, attentive partner
- Helping others improve their quality of life
- Making enough money to provide for her family's future

Could she meet these needs by becoming a yoga instructor? Very possibly. Is that the only job that could meet her interests? Certainly not.

Simply put, interests yield multiple options while positions do not. A detailed awareness of your interests will make it much easier for you to broaden your thinking about what might actually satisfy all of your most important interests. This kind of open-minded, creative approach to meeting your interests will help you broaden your job and lifestyle prospects.

Identifying interests is also essential if you run into roadblocks when seeking an "ideal" job. When you get "positional," you lose the ability to adapt, as Laura found when she learned that the yoga instructor market in her area was saturated. Were she to focus on her basic motivators—her interests—Laura would stand a better chance of meeting those interests in another way, such as by becoming a certified personal trainer. Or maybe, after looking at her interests, she could decide to become a realtor: It helps meet her financial obligations, it gives her a more flexible schedule, and while it's not as active as teaching yoga, she's out and about showing properties rather than sitting behind a desk. It would also give her greater insight into the broader dynamics of housing in her area. And she could still deepen her involvement in the yoga community by offering occasional free classes to friends and colleagues, or at her partner's organization, thereby laying the groundwork for possibly becoming a professional yoga instructor later on.

Thinking about your career development in an interest-based way by no means implies either settling for less or seeking perfection at the expense of more modest satisfaction. Instead, it's about giving serious and open thought to what's driving you so that you can find satisfaction and fulfillment in what you do professionally.

It's All About the Why

Your conversations with yourself are all about figuring out what you want from your work so that you can look for jobs that fulfill those needs really well. People sometimes get stuck at this stage either because they can't pick a field to learn more about or because they pick a specific job, sometimes even at a specific business, and focus narrowly on that job rather than understanding what it is about it that appeals to them, and then using that knowledge as the filter for considering what field to go into.

So, your conversations with yourself are all about figuring out what you want from your work so that you can look for jobs that fulfill those needs really well, but how do you figure out what those interests are? Exercise 1 will guide you to identify what your current interests are. In the first part, you will practice thinking expansively to identify kinds of work that are attractive, fulfilling, or meaningful to you. In the second part, you will think through the reasons why you're drawn to them, and then look for patterns. At the end, you'll have the first glimpse of your interests!

You'll develop lists of interests in Exercises 2 and 3 as well, using different ways to discover them and finding different categories of interests. It's from those lists that you'll generate your Interest Profile. You might feel unsure of yourself when you're doing these exercises at first, but with the practice you get through doing them, your new interest spotting skills will begin to emerge.

Keep in mind that you can come back to this exercise, or any of the others, anytime they would be helpful again—next week or next year. Actually, next week *and* next year, since as time passes some of your interests will change. You're under no pressure to think of everything that matters to you on the first pass. If you miss something important, it will surface later on, during your conversations with connectors.

Thinking Expansively: EXERCISE 1

This exercise will inspire creative thinking about what you could do with your work life. Being able to think about your career creatively is essential. The activities can be done all at once—although that would make for an intense day of self-reflection—or you can spread them out. Altogether, they will take you about 60 to 90 minutes—plus whatever breaks you need to recharge. We suggest that you read through the exercise first and then decide how to proceed.

Because this exercise is designed to bring out big ideas, it's nice to do it in spaces that inspire big thinking for you. That might be somewhere outside, or it could be while listening to epic music. Perhaps it's in a quiet corner of a library where you can shut out the rest of the world and think. All you need to have with you is Worksheet 1.

You can do this exercise on your own. However, we find that if you complete it with a friend or trusted colleague who is also wanting to stretch and think big, the combined creativity can lead to a richer set of ideas.

To get things going, allow yourself to stretch into a mindset of freedom and agency. You want to make sure not to limit your thinking in any way—embrace even ideas that seem absurdly unlikely.* For a lot of people, this will take some getting used to.

---

* Inspiration for this exercise came from the concept of dreamlining, which is from Timothy Ferriss's *The 4-Hour Workweek* (New York: Crown, 2007), 57–63.

EXERCISE 1 WORKSHEET

THINKING EXPANSIVELY

Scan QR Code or visit
findingajobthatlovesyouback.com
for the free downloadable worksheet

PURPOSE:	To inspire creative thinking about what you might want to do with your work life and then uncover the underlying needs that inform what you are drawn to
RESULT:	A list of your interests drawn from thinking about kinds of work you find exciting
TIME:	60 to 90 Minutes
PREPARATION:	Time and a space that helps you feel relaxed and creative, and, if you like, a buddy
INSTRUCTIONS:	Pages 38–44

PART 1
PRACTICE THINKING EXPANSIVELY

PART 2
**UNCOVERING THE INTERESTS
BEHIND YOUR IDEAS**

PART 3
FINDING PATTERNS

As adults, we rarely let our imaginations fly like this. Most of us fall out of the habit of dreaming of becoming an astronaut, a paleontologist, or a superhero unicorn when we're still in elementary school, so this exercise can be challenging. It may feel silly or hard—or both—to think about your career without focusing on—or even considering—constraints and immediate practicality. We know, though, based on our own experiences and working with clients, that once you get past the initial discomfort, thinking expansively will revive some of your meaningful old dreams and bring new ones to the surface. The goal here isn't to encourage something that's unreasonable, like getting you to quit everything and take up gymnastics for the first time since eighth grade in a bid for an Olympic medal. It's opening your mind to possibility, because thinking expansively is essential for approaching your career in a creative way.

Part 1:
Practice Thinking Expansively

Answer each of the following questions that capture your imagination. Feel free to skip any that don't call to you. This part of the exercise will take 15 to 30 minutes. The idea here is not to actually plan your career but to help you notice what kinds of work you feel drawn to so that you can look for themes and patterns in what sparks your excitement. At the end of this part of the exercise, compile your answers into a single list of work interests. Be as open minded as possible. At this stage, do your best to avoid analyzing your answers.

- Think back to previous jobs, internships, or volunteer experiences you enjoyed. Which ones were the most interesting and engaging?
- Think about your friends, family, and community. What jobs do people you know have that you admire, respect, and think would be engaging for you?
- Think about movies, books, TV, and social media. Have you come across any jobs there and thought to yourself, "It would be awesome if I could do that!"?

These don't have to be real jobs at all. If you think being a wizard or a space navigator would be awesome, definitely write it down.

- Imagine winning the lottery. You'll never have to work for money again, but you want to build a career that makes you eager to start every day and that gives you a sense of purpose. What are some of the things you would do?

- Imagine that your success at anything you attempted was guaranteed and that no one would disapprove of what you did. In this scenario, if you opened a restaurant where everyone does crossword puzzles, every patron would love it, your family would think it was the best idea ever, and you would easily make enough money to cover your expenses. In this world of total acceptance and success, what kinds of things would you do?

You may wonder why it's worth thinking about what to do if you won the lottery or could not fail. Maybe you would buy an island and protect its ecosystem—but you don't live in that world (and we don't either) so how is that information helpful? In the next part of this exercise, you'll take all of your ideas, from the most mundane to the most outlandish, and examine them to discover what it is about each idea that appeals to you. Becoming a space explorer or starting your own restaurant might not be very likely. But if you can find out what it is about those ideas that inspires you, you can use that insight to think of other jobs out there that are achievable and meet those same interests.

For example, let's imagine that the thing about being a space explorer that appeals to you is learning things no one else has known before, and what you like about the idea of starting your own restaurant is sharing your enthusiasm and keeping morale up while doing something truly challenging. Those seemingly extreme or just-too-risky ideas have given you two criteria to look for in your job search: a role that involves exploring the unknown and one where you get to support and bolster a team doing something difficult. There are lots of jobs that could meet those needs that don't involve the perils of starting a restaurant or of going into space.

Part 2:
Uncovering the Interests Behind Your Ideas

Now comes the fun part! You get to examine all the possible jobs you listed above for underlying interests that make work meaningful for you, which will take about 30 to 45 minutes. Pick one of the jobs you wrote down in Part 1 that excites you, and answer the question: What about this job appeals to me? Write out a few characteristics. From there, go on to the next job and answer the same question. Take a break or come back to this later if you start to run out of steam. As much fun as this is, it can take some real energy, too.

Part 3:
Finding Patterns

Now that you have a list of reasons why each idea appealed to you, read through what you wrote down under each job and look for patterns. This will take you about 15 minutes. What interests appear several times?

Here is an example of what this exercise looked like for one person's first round. It will give you a sense of what it can look like.

Example Part 1:
Practice Thinking Expansively

- Previous jobs, internships, or volunteer experiences
    - Supporting people who are creating inviting and engaging events about social justice issues
    - Working with preschoolers to increase literacy skills
    - Organizing with marginalized people to get stuff done, but from the background
- Jobs of friends and family, and in your community
    - (Not answered)
- Jobs from movies, books, TV, and social media—not necessarily real jobs

- Researching supernatural creatures or wacky happenings to help the people who keep people safe from them, but not actually being on the front lines fighting them
- Win the lottery and have a sense of purpose
  - Build interactive, fun, and educational games about social justice issues
  - Co-lead discussion groups about various social justice topics for learners who just need a little bit of structure but have the motivation
  - Run transformative justice circles
- Success at anything, with zero disapproval
  - Run a sanctuary for rabbits
  - Design and share a set of games that help people recover from trauma

Example Part 2:
Uncovering the Interests Behind Your Ideas

Here are three examples of answering the question, "What about this job appeals to me?"

- Supporting people who are creating inviting and engaging events about social justice issues
  - Being a supportive person for others running events
  - Being in the background but integral to the execution of events
  - Not getting any attention for this, only acknowledgment from the people who know I do background work—not having any fuss made over me
- Working with preschoolers to increase literacy skills
  - Working with children as they grow and learn
  - Being a part of their socialization at a young age— showing them how many different kinds of people exist

- Becoming a part of a child's world—building a relationship with them
- Learning (and teaching) through play!
- Organizing with marginalized people to get stuff done (but from the background)
  - Love doing strategy work!
  - Working one-on-one, building relationships and understanding the *why* for people who organize to help motivate them in hard times
  - Telling stories and using them to engage and involve people in meaningful work.
  - Working with people who have similar values and a healthy combo of realism and optimism for a world that we can create!
  - Tangible differences—even small wins are wins!

Example Part 3:
Finding Patterns

Looking through all the answers to the question "What about this job excites me?" across all of the roles, some patterns emerge in this example. The person who completed this exercise would be happy in a job where they would get to

- Support meaningful work but from the background
- Do design work that supports learning and teaching through play/games
- Directly support people who have suffered emotional harm
- Build relationships, both one-on-one and in community

Creating this short bullet list is your goal in the exercise.

Note that this person didn't answer one of the questions. Everyone's experiences and paths are different, so it only makes sense that everyone's exercise responses will be different. Allow yourself to move on if it feels like you're trying to force an answer. Maybe one will come to you later. And maybe not. Just follow your enthusiasm, and your creative momentum will only pick up.

Revealing Interests by Reframing

After you've completed this first exercise, with your proto–Interest Profile in hand, you can start having constructive conversations with connectors who have a broader understanding of the working world than you do to get their ideas on what jobs and careers might meet the set of interests that you have discovered through this exercise. It can be tempting to want to fixate on a particular job/career right away. This gives a sense of certainty and direction. If you can, resist the temptation to commit to a particular direction until you have had the chance to talk with a few connectors about your interests and found out what they think might be a good fit for you.

Now it's time to implement one of the core competencies of a skilled negotiator: reframing. In this case, the aim is to reframe your aspirations and your memories of past achievements (and failures) as interests that you can satisfy.

In his book *Getting Past No*, William Ury defines reframing as a conscious redirection of attention.* In a negotiation context, we're trying to redirect attention away from positions and toward interests. Reframing is first and foremost a practice in thinking about different contexts and approaching something from different angles.

Tad has a couple of examples to help demystify reframing.

> *TAD:* When I was a senior in college, I wanted to take up a new activity, but I didn't have any idea what it would be. A friend, let's call him Joel, asked me what I like to do. I blurted out, "I love to ski!" Joel, who had skied with me, understood and asked, "Why do you like to ski?" I hadn't really thought about it before and eventually replied, "I love the feeling of a set of perfect turns, focusing on one thing, continuously improving, getting outside on cold days, being with a group of friends, and the sense of accomplishment looking back up at a tough run I just came down. Also,

* William Ury, *Getting Past No: Negotiating in Difficult Situations* (New York: Bantam, 1991), 78.

I actually relax when I ski." Joel smiled and offered, "It sounds like you're looking for something that will feel great with good technique; enable you to focus, be present, improve, and relax; give you a reason to get outside and be with friends; and provide you with a sense of accomplishing something when you're done." The mindset switch from what I liked about *skiing* to what I wanted in *any activity* opened up a bunch of ideas, which led me to take up golf soon after, and later, to go on a guided monthlong group hiking trip in Alaska.

In the example above, Joel asking Tad why he likes to ski is similar to someone saying they want to be an office manager and then asking themselves, "Why do I want to be an office manager?" They then identify the interests behind being an office manager, which is the reframe.

TAD: A different type of reframing happened when my wife and I were moving to the Boston area and looking for a house. We had set up an appointment with a realtor, Peggy, to look at houses. When we got in her car, Peggy said, "You're probably not going to like the first few houses." In fact, she was right, and after the third house my wife, Betsy, asked, "Why are you taking us to houses we don't like? They're all either too dark inside, or the kitchen's too small, or there aren't enough trees, or there's no yard for the kids to play in, or no fireplaces." Peggy replied, "Well, I now have a pretty good list of what you want. You're looking for a house that's bright inside, with a good-sized kitchen, at least one fireplace, lots of trees, and a big yard, plus a family room with character, a place for a workshop, and possibly a finished attic space for an office. I'm pretty confident you're going to like the next houses!"

We are asking you to reframe positions as interests because lim-iting yourself to a single position reduces agility and adaptability and conceals options. Thinking about Laura's situation, if she can only see one path, she will live in a binary world of either becoming a yoga instructor or "failing." To negotiate effectively, you want to exercise the skill of shifting contexts and perceptions to ensure that you're seeing the most that you can see and getting the most out of your negotiation with yourself. You want to view your initial positions as clues to your interests.

To help you negotiate with yourself about your career aspirations, we use reframing in two major ways. (1) by having you ask yourself *why* your activities, accomplishments, and aspirations are so appealing to you, and (2) by having you shift your focus from past negatives to future positives (for example, from "My boss never trusts me" to "I want my boss to trust me"). All of this is leading up to developing your Interest Profile—that concrete list of interests. Figuring out how best to meet these interests will guide you in deciding what career moves to make and what career path to map out.

And now, some practice.

Reframing Activities as Interests: EXERCISE 2

This exercise takes about half an hour, and it can be done solo or with others. We recommend that you do it once by yourself at first, and then invite others to do it with you later if you like. If you work with another person, we recommend that one of you reads the instructions out loud and that each of you records your own responses.

Use Worksheet 2 for the three steps in this exercise.

Step 1: Activities

In column 1, list all of the activities in your life—personal or work-related—that give you a sense of flow. *Flow* means that the activity comes easily, is enjoyable, and gives you a sense of meaning. It gets you going. When people are "in flow," they become totally immersed in the activity, sometimes to the point of losing track of time. Flow might include feeling capable, alive, confident, effective,

EXERCISE 2 WORKSHEET

REFRAMING ACTIVITIES AS INTERESTS

Scan QR Code or visit
findingajobthatlovesyouback.com
for the free downloadable worksheet

PURPOSE: To get more comfortable with thinking in terms of interests and to build your reframing skills

RESULT: A list of process and outcome interests met through doing activities that give you a sense of flow

TIME: 30 minutes

PREPARATION: None

INSTRUCTIONS: Pages 47–50

ACTIVITIES	OUTCOME INTERESTS	PROCESS INTERESTS

fulfilled, impressive, proud, or any other feelings of empowerment.

The activities you record can be anything from making others laugh to building a city out of Legos, or from skiing to figuring out how to file your own taxes.

Step 2: Interests Met by the Outcomes

Now, in column 2 write down what you get out of the outcomes of the activity. What is it about the results of those activities that is important to you? Here are some possible examples.

- A sense of personal accomplishment
- Recognition from others
- Proving you could do it
- Financial stability
- A sense of helping others or giving back
- Feeling like you built or created something of value
- Contributing to positive changes in the world
- Prevailing over difficulty, insecurity, or frustration

Step 3: Interests Met by the Process

In column 3, try to capture what was important about the *doing* of the activities you listed in column 1. How would you describe what you like about the process of doing that activity? What is meaningful to you about the way that activity is carried out? Why do you enjoy doing it? How would you describe the way you arrived at the interest you listed in column 2? Some examples could be:

- Working with your hands
- Striving to find solutions
- Feeling a sense of adventure
- Conducting analysis
- Working independently
- Building consensus
- Making a strong connection with another individual

What you've written in columns 2 and 3 are the interests that underlie your sense of flow!

Since reframing like this will be useful to you many times in the future, make a mental note now not to forget that even the activities you enjoy in your personal life likely reflect the sorts of interests that would make a career fulfilling for you.

Flexing Your Reframing Muscles: EXERCISE 3

This exercise lets you hone your reframing skills and identify more career-related interests to add to your Interest Profile. It's one you'll want to do more than once because it's great practice. You'll likely want to repeat it over time, even once you have a robust Interest Profile, too. That's because what you'll be reframing later is different from what you're reframing now. For example, we hope you get to a point in your career where you're starting to itch for a change but you're not sure why because you feel like your situation is pretty great. Reframing is how you'll figure that out. Also, you may want to do this exercise with one other person sooner or later. It takes up to half an hour.

This type of reframing takes a statement and recasts it in a new light. The examples below show two approaches: shifting from

- negative to positive, and
- past focused to future focused.

Step 1:
Reframing Prep

Read over the following example statements related to a hypothetical job hunt. Notice how the reframed versions make the two shifts.

Statement 1: I just can't spend another day alone, staring at a computer screen for eight hours!

Reframed statement: I want an engaging work life that involves other people and a variety of work tasks or modes (maybe working meetings, drafting by hand, reasonable screen time, etc.)

Statement 2: My last boss was a terror. He never listened to my feedback, and after a while I just stopped sharing my ideas. I used to love thinking about design and fashion. Now I just feel like avoiding it altogether.

Reframed statement: I hope to find an environment where my work is appreciated and I'm rewarded for thinking creatively, and where I get to do work I feel passionate about.

Statement 3: The principal investigator at my lab told me I would never succeed if I struck out on my own. I'm worried that she might be right. My last venture failed, and I can't afford to take the financial risk at this point.

Reframed statement: I'm looking for a chance to do something innovative and independent in a way that preserves my financial security.

In all of these statements, the reframed version takes the same desires that are being expressed in the original statement and recasts them to focus on the *future* and on the *positive*. They are positively repurposed.

Step 2:
Practice Reframing Career-Related Statements

Now read the questions below and write your answers on Worksheet 3. These questions are meant to help you define your career development and/or job search up to this point. (If you're very early in your career, use your educational experiences to answer these questions.)

1. What was a specific career-related project, task, assignment, or moment that you really enjoyed, and why?
2. What was a specific career-related project, task, assignment, or moment that you really disliked, and why?
3. When were you the happiest with your overall career situation, and why?
4. When were you the most dissatisfied with your overall career situation, and why?

EXERCISE 3 WORKSHEET

FLEXING YOUR REFRAMING MUSCLES

Scan QR Code or visit findingajobthatlovesyouback.com for the free downloadable worksheet

PURPOSE: To make reframing something you can do easily and naturally

RESULT: Five specifically career-related interests that are positive and focused on the future

TIME: 30 minutes

PREPARATION: None, or inviting someone (a peer) so you can do the exercise together

INSTRUCTIONS: Pages 50–53

ANSWER	POSITIVE, FUTURE-FOCUSED REFRAME

5. What statement or phrase —either general or specific —
describes your work history so far?

After you've answered these five questions, read your statements
carefully and underline any sections that are past focused, negative
(focused on what you *don't* want), or that lead to only one or very few
options (meaning they're positional). Then reframe your statements,
making each of the underlined sections future focused and positive
(focused on what you *do* want).

When you're doing this exercise with a partner, resist the temptation to sit in silence while you're trying to reframe each other's
answers. It takes time to develop the habit of thinking this way
before it becomes second nature. Work collaboratively on each
one. Think through them aloud, helping each other work through
the process of reframing. Do your partner's attempts at reframing
your statements actually capture your real interests? Some things
will likely get lost in translation as you make your first attempts at
reframing. Use these opportunities to talk through what you were
trying to say and discuss different ways of phrasing your reframed
statements to get closer to your meaning. Be open to interests your
partner might identify in your statements that you didn't realize you
had.

When you've completed this exercise, your reframed statements
will reflect some of your genuine, career-related interests. On its
own, this exercise isn't meant to create an exhaustive list of your
interests. Rather, it is designed to help you improve your ability to
reframe in order to identify more and more of them with increasing
ease.

Everyday Reframing Practice

Over the next days and weeks, keep this skill of reframing in mind,
and practice it any chance you get. We'll refer back to it throughout
the book, too. For instance, once you're in Phase 3 and speaking to
a possible employer, if they mention things that haven't gone well in
the past, you'll be able to process what they've said and reframe on
the spot. By articulating what it is your potential employer does want

going forward, you can align whatever you are proposing with what they need—make sure it meets the interests you have uncovered.

> *Employer:* We've had some brilliant people working here at Hippogriff Emporium, Inc., but a lot of them were very young and didn't really know what they wanted. Too many employees were busy trying to create start-ups on the side, and some took off after a few months to work in a totally different field. We couldn't grow or innovate!
>
> *You:* So what you're looking for is people who can commit and focus their energy on helping the company grow. I'm glad to hear that because I'm looking for an organization where I can dig in and help shape its future. In fact . . .

Being able to reframe a potential employer's comments to articulate their interests *and describe how you can meet those interests*, will make your conversations and negotiations much more likely to be interest-based and productive.

Creating the First Edition of Your Interest Profile

Now, with a robust interest list—a list of your biggest dreams and your outcome and process interests—and a better understanding of reframing and future-focused interests, you can create your Interest Profile!

Start by opening or laying out Worksheets 1, 2, and 3, and opening a new document or, if you prefer, a spreadsheet. Review the Worksheets as a group so you have all of the ground you've covered fresh in your mind. Then focus on the Exercise 1 Worksheet, Part 3, and on your blank Interest Profile, add your list of common themes that emerged behind your broad and creative thinking. Review that list and consider which process interests to add to it that you uncovered in Exercise 2, Reframing Activities as Interests. After making these additions, your Interest Profile should directly answer two questions: "What do I want to get out of my working life?" and "How do I want my working life to be?" With these two questions answered, the next piece is to add the career interests you uncovered by answering and reframing the five questions in Step 2 of Exercise 3, Flexing Your Reframing Muscles. The last task is to use the reframing skill you built during Exercise 3 to review all of the interests you have listed and ensure they are all framed in a way that is positive and future focused. All of your interests should be phrased in a way that they can complete the sentence that begins, "What I want going forward is: . . . ." With this final adjustment, you have a working Interest Profile that you can now begin to test out and refine in your conversations with connectors.

If there are clear patterns that emerge among your interests, you might want to subcategorize your list, combining "process interests," "education/training interests," "relationship/interaction interests," and so on to help you home in on what's important to you. Ensuring that your interests at the center of your career conversations will enable you to be creative and flexible in your career development while still holding true to what is most important to you. You will be using your Interest Profile in a slightly different way at each phase of the book. In the next chapter, you will use your first conversations with connectors to quality control this first list you have created. Once you are confident in your own interests, it is time to shift your focus to figuring out what the core interests are of those in the industry you want to succeed in. This is the primary work of Phase 2, Increasing Access. With a clear understanding of your interests and the interests of the decision makers in the field you are entering, you will have the information you need to start negotiating with decision makers. You will want to put their interests at the center of your proposals to them, even as you make proposals that meet your core interests.

It's important to note here that while you're working on gaining clarity with your Interest Profile, you'll definitely be considering your work-life balance, and the interests you discover—or rediscover—by doing the exercises will naturally be related to your personal life. As you review and revise your Interest Profile going

forward, make sure to prioritize the interests that are most important for you to meet through your job. Your job can't satisfy every
one of your interests, nor do you want it to. It's important to have
clarity on which ones would be better met in other areas of your life,
or even in the future rather than right now.

As a working, ever-evolving document, your Interest Profile will
help define your career path. You'll use it to: help your connectors
give you useful advice, decide which opportunities to pursue, and
advocate for yourself in your collaborative negotiations with decision makers. The significant shift to thinking in terms of interests
is what unlocks your capacity to turn just about every career-related
conversation you have into a collaborative effort—a conversation
about meeting someone else's interests in a way that will also meet
yours. As you proceed with the rest of the journey described in this
book, you will develop the skill of picking up on interests, yours and
others'. Becoming able to listen to people's initial proposals, coun-
ter arguments, and concerns, and to hear in them their underlying interests, is the most important skill you can acquire to become
good at finding jobs that will love you back.

2

Bringing Out Your Story

It's almost time to reach out to connectors (the second of the three conversations), people with career experience, to get their advice on where to go from here, and to benefit from their wisdom and perspectives. Turning your Interest Profile into a story that you can share with them will help you do this effectively.

At this stage, connectors will be helping you confirm and refine your interests and get a wide-angle perspective on how your interests connect to the work world. In addition to broadening your perspective by talking to connectors, you'll also be seeking to create a list of professional possibilities that you'll pursue in the last section of Phase 1, Finding Clarity.

Who makes a good Phase 1 connector? Probably people you already know. That way, it's easier to set up a meeting (which at this point may be as casual as getting together for coffee or just chatting on a video call) and, more importantly, if they already know you it's easier for them to give you feedback on your interests and career ideas. Ideally, they have broad professional and life experience and are happy to help you develop your story. Thanks to their worldliness, good Phase 1 connectors are the ones who are in a position to suggest work or training options that correspond to your interests, and who can also foresee potential roadblocks or challenges you might face in achieving your goals. Of course, to get the most from your interactions with connectors in Phase 1—as well as in the later phases—you'll need to be clear about how you'd like these people to help you and how you can negotiate for their help.

What you're asking for from connectors will change over the course of this phase. You might start by asking for them to reality-check your interests: How do the interests you've described line up with what they know about you? As you get more comfortable with your list of interests, connectors will be able to shed light on career options that could fulfill those interests. From there, a few specific options will begin to catch your attention. When that happens, you can ask what they know about the details of day-to-day work in those jobs or fields.

In theory, almost anyone can act as a connector. Often, conversations with connectors in Phase 1 are informal and unrehearsed; they may happen in someone's kitchen, at a barbeque, or during a gathering after work. Still, we want to provide a structure for these conversations that you can use if you get stuck. We encourage you to talk to as many people as possible about how they got to where they are, what they love and regret about their career paths, and, most importantly, what they would do if they were in your shoes.

Forging Your Story with Others

Getting connected to a new direction or field requires a bit of due diligence. Take Louis's situation as an example.

Louis largely enjoyed his eight years as an electrician. Much of his work had involved kneeling or working overhead for long hours, though, and he could already tell that it was taking a toll on his back and knees. So he started thinking about doing something less physically strenuous. He'd always been good at working with numbers, and he decided to go back to school for a degree in accounting.

His only problem was that he knew next to nothing about the world of accounting. In fact, he didn't even know if he really wanted to be an accountant. He was aware of the stereotype that accounting could be mindless and boring, but he was hopeful that this cliché didn't reflect reality. "Accountant" was the job he associated with having a knack for numbers, though, and he did know he had that.

Louis started by reading what he could online about being an accountant and about how to get trained and certified. Based on his findings, he applied to several accounting programs in his region so that he wouldn't have to uproot his life. He got accepted to one, dove right into his classes, and did well. And then he graduated, having spent tens of thousands of dollars on an education, only to soon discover that finding a job as an accountant was a huge hurdle.

Applying for jobs was onerous and time consuming, and he didn't really know what potential employers actually looked for in new hires. He didn't get any callbacks. And then his attempts to work as an independent accountant failed because he didn't have an established client base or industry references.

At this point, Louis felt alone and started to second-guess his choice. A career in accounting still felt far away. He had the feeling that he still had so much to figure out before his career could advance. Louis hadn't necessarily made a bad career move, but like Laura in the previous chapter, he had focused on a single idea without identifying what kind of accounting job he wanted or whether accounting would actually meet his interests. Even after getting trained as an accountant, he still had only a vague understanding of the landscape of the field and the broader ecosystem of industries and skills associated with accounting. As a result, he was having a hard time changing course and figuring out his next move.

Louis did good research online to figure out how to become qualified as an accountant. What he missed were tips about how to start working in the accounting world and the importance of relationship building during school. This too he could have found out through online research if he had known to ask these questions. The challenge is knowing what questions we should be asking. A few conversations might have given him a more realistic understanding of the challenges in going from accounting graduate to employed accountant and spurred him to spend more time building relationships with potential employers during his degree program.

One way he could have learned more about the field would have been to talk to accountants about how they got into that field and whether they thought there were realistic job prospects for accounting jobs that met his personal interests. Another possibility would have been to interview his professors about how to make the most of his time in school. Or, he might have uncovered similar options that perhaps better fit his interests, such as becoming a sports statistician or an actuary. He would also have done well to talk to anyone else in arms reach that had made a mid-life career change. What kinds of lessons or revelations would they have given him?

How to Build a Story That Inspires

We're here to help you avoid the pitfalls that Louis encountered. In our experience, there are two steps to building a story that inspires: (1) construct a well-developed story and (2) have conversations with as many connectors as you can. They go hand in hand.

Connectors not only hold the information you need to match your interests with a field, they can also provide important feedback about the effectiveness of your story. They can help you by sharing their stories, connecting you with others, and giving you advice. To get the most out of each conversation you will have to define your story, by weaving your Interest Profile into a compelling narrative and adjusting it as you go based on the information and feedback you receive from connectors.

Your Interest Profile is currently in the form of a list. But lists aren't nearly as compelling as a good narrative, so an essential next step is to pull your interests together into an engaging story. Here, we walk you through an exercise that will help you figure out the content of your story and how to tell it.

Writing Your Story: EXERCISE 4

This exercise will guide you as you develop the story you will share with connectors about you and your interests before you ask for their advice. The goal is to frame your interests with compelling contextual information that will focus your connectors so they can give you useful advice.

In the first sections of the exercise, all you will need is your Interest Profile and Worksheet 4. In the later sections, where you will be sharing your story and getting feedback, you will need a listener who can be your sounding board. We recommend someone who knows you well and from whom you feel comfortable taking feedback.

In our experience doing this exercise with coaching clients, it usually takes about an hour to draft, share, and revise.

Part 1: Drafting Your Story

Your story will be made up of five parts: biographical information, passion, interests, constraints, and a call for support. To begin bringing out your story, write out answers to each of the following prompts.

1. Biographical Information

Create a list of relevant biographical information about yourself: where you're from, what kinds of work you've done so far, what you do for fun, languages you speak, where you went to school, where you volunteer, what kind of music you like, etc.

From this list, put a star next to the three pieces of biographical information that are most relevant to your work-related interests and desired career path (if you know it already). Circle two pieces of biographical information that you feel make you particularly interesting or unique. You will want to focus on what's starred and circled in your final narrative.

The biographical information that you end up including in your story should be information that relates to your career and helps the connector get a feel for how you got to your current situation. That being said, it's also worth including more personal tidbits if you feel they will help you make a connection with a particular connector or if they'll help make you especially memorable.

EXERCISE 4 WORKSHEET

WRITING YOUR STORY

Scan QR Code or visit
findingajobthatlovesyouback.com
for the free downloadable worksheet

PURPOSE: To develop the story you will share with connectors about you and your interests to channel their advice toward what will be most helpful to you

RESULT: A compelling story that clarifies for connectors what interests you are hoping to meet and what obstacles you need to overcome to meet them

TIME: 60 minutes

PREPARATION: Your Interest Profile for Part 1 and a partner for Part 3

INSTRUCTIONS: Pages 60–68

PART 1
DRAFTING YOUR STORY

PART 2
PUTTING IT ALL TOGETHER

PART 3
PRACTICE

2. Passion

What gets you fired up? What kind of positive change do you want to create in your community, country, or in the world? What is it that drives you to wake up every day and face the world?

Start out by completing this statement: "I want to live in a world where . . ." Then complete that sentence several more times, each time highlighting a different aspect of the world you want to live in. You might want a world free from diabetes, or one where you never have to worry about housing or money again, or where professional academics take an active role in making their research applicable to day-to-day corporate operations. Choose a different angle each time. For instance: How do people interact? What is the physical world like? How does society use technology? How do members of the global community relate? How are privacy, safety, and security handled? What is the financial system like?

Pick the sentence that feels the best to you—the most alive, the most accurate, the most urgent, the most interesting, whatever it may be. This will help you explain to others why you care about what you care about. Choose the statement that has the most positive emotional charge for you. The point of including your passion is to bring contagious enthusiasm to your story.

3. Interests

Go back to your Interest Profile, mark the interests that are most vital to you, and transfer those to your Worksheet. If any interests now seem more important to you than when you first wrote them down, put a star next to them on your Worksheet so you can highlight them when you share your story.

4. Constraints

Think about the factors that will most influence the decisions you make about your future career and write a list. Do you have a certain income or geography requirement? Do you have other requirements about your work life, like being outdoors, working nights, or not needing a car to get to work? Do you have such a severe shark phobia that you don't think you could handle working within 100 miles of any coast?

Which of these constraints are nonnegotiable and which could you possibly work around? Circle the constraints over which you have very little control, like remaining in a particular city to care for elderly relatives. Leave uncircled the constraints that, under the right circumstances, you might be able to approach with flexibility, such as taking courses.

5. Call for Support

You eventually want to ask connectors for help in identifying and advancing your next step. During Phases 1 and 2 you'll want to be clear with them that you are looking for general advice about meeting your interests, not specific information about open job postings. In our coaching work, we've found that connectors at this stage often assume that you're looking for specific job openings, regardless of what you say. So make sure to specify what you are asking for. Often, the question is something like, "If you were me, what would you do?"

People tend to overthink the call for support, but it's almost always best to keep it simple. The only reason to deviate from "If you were me, what would you do?" is to focus the connector on a specific interest or type of support. For example, if you wanted to focus your connector on helping you get more informational interviews, you might ask, "If you were me, who are the other people you would most want to connect with to get more insight into how this field works?" If you wanted advice specifically on your interests around being able to travel for work, you might ask, "If you were me, considering what's important to me, what would you do if you wanted to travel a lot?"

Think about each connector you'll be having a conversation with and decide whether "If you were me, what would you do?" is a good enough question—it probably is. If you do need to focus the connector a little more, write down the secondary calls for support you might want to make that are specific to that person. Additional examples of specific questions for connectors are provided in the "Questions for Your Connector" section on page 72.

Part 2: Putting It All Together

To help you put all the pieces together and write your first story draft, here is an example of a draft version of Carly's story, which they put together prior to meeting with one of their connectors, a psychotherapist, during their own Phase 1 progress. This is meant to serve as a rough guide in terms of length and detail. Your story will become your own and start to flow naturally as you get used to telling and tweaking it. Here's Carly.

> *CARLY'S STORY:* Nice to meet you. Thanks for taking the time to meet me. [*Biographical Information:*] I've been working in Boston for the past four years, in all sorts of different jobs, but I'm still trying to figure out exactly what career I should be doing. I studied English and biology in college, and I've worked in communications and done some work related to fish farming, but none of that has been a great fit for me. [*Passion:*] I've recently been trained as a mediator and I really enjoy working with people. But I've been getting the feeling that I'm more interested in exploring the psychology underneath people's conflicts, instead of doing one-time mediations to solve a dispute. It's like something is still missing for me with mediation. I never studied psychology in school, but I've been doing some reading and I've completely fallen in love with it! [*Interests:*] More concretely, I'm trying to figure out what other jobs are out there where I could work with people one on one in a more in-depth way than I do as a mediator. [*Constraints:*] I'm not planning to go back to school right now, but I'm hoping to go to grad school within the next few years. [*Call for Support:*] I'd love to learn more about why you chose to be a social worker, what your job is like day to day, and if it might be a good fit for me.

Part 3:
Practice Telling and Tweaking Your Story

After you've created a written version of your story, it's time to practice telling it. Writing down your narrative is an excellent start, but
the purpose of your story is to help to seek advice and eventually
opportunities. In order for the story to be useful, you have to get
comfortable sharing it with others. It's important that you practice
with someone in real time so that you get feedback on how your
story comes across in a real-life conversation and learn to incorpo-
rate others' advice into your narrative.

For this part of the exercise, you'll need to recruit a sympathetic
listener, like a close friend or family member, so that you can ask
them for their feedback on your story. If you feel more comfortable
in a group setting, gather a few people to do this exercise with.

Narrative Version

Once you have a partner to help you out, the first step is to read the
written version aloud to them. It will probably feel a little stilted
to read a written story about yourself, but it's good practice. After
you've read your story, ask your listener for feedback. What did they
find most compelling about it? What sparked their curiosity? What
made them most interested in possibly supporting or helping you?
Are there things that didn't make sense or things that seemed to be
missing? After you've had a chance to discuss the written version
together, move on to working on the conversational version.

Conversational Version

To practice sharing your story in a more natural, back-and-forth
conversational format, have your listener ask you these questions:
- What's your background?
- What are you passionate about?
- What are your career-related interests?
- What are your constraints?
- What support are you asking for?

Your goal here is to practice answering these questions as naturally as possible, in a casual, conversational way. At this point, try not to worry about how your answers sound. Nothing is at stake. Your aim is just to get comfortable sharing the main points of your story.

After you answer all the questions, you and your listener can discuss how your conversational answers compared to your scripted story. Consider these questions:

- How well do the two versions align?
- Are there important points or compelling phrases in the conversational version that didn't make it into the initial telling of the story, or vice versa?
- Did the written story feel as natural as the conversational version?
- What was compelling about each?
- What could have been better in each?
- Did the listener hear specific and important interests that weren't named in the written story?
- Did the listener hear more than they needed to, or not enough?

The objective of this part of the exercise is to ensure that your story truly captures what you want to say. As you first get used to creating and telling your story, it's easy to end up with either an awkward or incomplete story, or with a story that is too brief or too long-winded to be meaningful. Testing out a conversational version with a sympathetic listener will give you a chance to figure out what you most want to say.

Revised Narrative

After you've practiced your story conversationally with another person, take some time on your own to rewrite your story, taking into account the feedback you've received so far. When you're done, you might want to send the updated written version to your listener and ask them for a final round of feedback.

At the end of this exercise, you will have a working story that you can use in your conversations with connectors.

When you're talking with connectors, you'll tell your story a little differently each time, depending on the context and the person you're speaking with. As you progress through the four phases in this book, you'll continually refine your story as you get more and more clarity about your career interests. As you learn about different possible career options, and as you think of more compelling ways to express yourself, and to enlist the help of connectors, your story will shift to reflect these changes.

Connectors: Starting Out

In general, helpful connectors in Phase 1 fall into three categories.

1. People who know you well. Perhaps these conversations emerged naturally during your self-reflection exercises in last chapter. Close family and friends may help clue you into talents you didn't realize you had, expose and clarify patterns in your behavior, or point you to new directions.

2. People who are familiar with a wide range of jobs and have experience helping people find professional direction. These might include volunteer alumni from your high school or college, career counselors, academic advisors, life or professional coaches, temp agencies, therapists, human resources professionals, recruiters, or representatives at career fairs. This list is a mix of professionals you may meet informally through your relationship-building and others who will expect to be paid. Some people have the means and find it helpful to engage paid professional help; others don't go this route. In chapter 5, which focuses on the conversation with connectors in Phase 2, we further discuss creative negotiation ideas to enlist the career mentoring and support you need from connectors.

3. People who have been through a similar transition to the one you are going through. Work colleagues who made a career jump, graduates from your alma mater who went into your desired career (when you know it), or people with a similar background who have a job that interests you could all fall within this category.

When seeking out connectors, first take stock of people you

already know, or know of, who seem like good candidates. To narrow it down, make a list of names generated from the following questions.

- Who do I know of who has a similar background to me and is a few years further ahead in their career development than I am? Perhaps they studied the same things I did in school, have a similar socioeconomic background, culture, personality, etc.
- Who do I know who understands me well, has seen me work in the past and might have ideas about how and where I might excel? These could be friends, family, mentors, previous employers, etc.

For those who already have clarity about their goals: Who do I know currently doing what I want to be doing? This can include personal contacts and role models, personal heroes, etc.

From these lists, circle the two people you feel most comfortable reaching out to for a conversation. Once you've spoken with both of them, go back to your list and circle the next two people with whom you feel most comfortable and set up meetings with them. Reaching out to connectors can be intimidating at first and just the thought of such a meeting might flood your mind with insecurities. We urge you to engage in the conversations despite any hesitations you might have. A few conversations with connectors can pave a significantly smoother career path for you. Whether you're intimidated or not at the thought of speaking to connectors, starting with your most comfortable connectors will help you work your way up to less familiar ones.

Approaching Conversations with Connectors

If you start out by contacting people you know, the likelihood of your catching and keeping their attention is naturally much higher. But as the people you know start to connect you to people *they* know, and those people start to connect you to others, pretty soon you'll be reaching out to strangers and asking them for their time. It is important that you do this in a way that maximizes your chances of getting a positive response and gaining an ally. At the same time, the more removed you are from the connector, the more formal the conversations typically become. If you are already finding yourself being referred to strangers, you might find it helpful to skip ahead to Chapter 5, "The Art of the Connector Conversation" in Phase 2.

The overall aim of these conversations is to expand your awareness of the possible ways to meet your career and life interests. At some point, discussing your interests will give way to a conversation about concrete options to meet those interests. How might your interests translate into real-world activities and gainful employment? What are the career paths that (directly or indirectly) correspond to your interests? Let's say you like working with kids, but there's no way you could stand being stuck in a classroom all day, so you don't want to become a teacher. What other realistic options are there to meet your interest of helping children?

In Phase 1, you're hoping to run across connectors who will push you to consider createive options, like opening a children's bookstore. You're also seeking connectors who can talk to you about the pros and cons of actual roles, like being a pediatrician or a summer camp director.

It's highly unusual for there to be just one way to meet a given set of interests, just as there is no single path into a field or profession. Sure, to be a lawyer, you need to pass the bar exam, and, in most states, to be accepted to the bar, you need a law degree. But there are many ways to get to law school and there are different kinds of legal educations and jobs available to those on a path to becoming a lawyer. What started out as a "lawyer path" might end up being the path of a conflict mediator, financial consultant, union representative, film producer, and so on.

At this stage, you may still need clarity on what is "adjacent" to the options you're already familiar with. Louis was aware that accounting was a possible "numbers job" and that it wasn't physically demanding. But there are many other kinds of numbers jobs that might have been a better fit for him. Most people are familiar with accountants; fewer people know what actuaries do. Well-known professions—like teacher, nurse, DJ, and store manager—provide a good jumping-off point for thinking about what types of jobs might be a good fit. But you don't want to get so focused on these familiar options that you neglect to explore lesser-known but related paths. At this stage, identifying even more options, or adjacencies, is one of your most important tasks. Exploring adjacencies will help add depth and flexibility to the ways you might meet your interests, and it will play a big part in your transition from your purpose in Phase 1: Finding Clarity to your purpose in Phase 2: Increasing Access.

Before you go into each conversation with a connector, take the time to clarify in your mind at least one thing you want to take away from the meeting. Here are four fallback purposes to keep in your back pocket that tend to apply to most conversations with Phase 1 connectors.

- To hear their story and think about whether or not their path appeals to you, given your interests and career ideas thus far.
- To better understand how hiring and advancement works in general (even if you don't have a specific field or job in mind yet).
- To bounce your ideas off the connector about what you want to do, would be good at, and would enjoy professionally.
- To practice telling your story.

The Conversation

When you start speaking with connectors, it is often helpful to open by asking them about how they came to do the work they are currently doing, and then share a version of your story—a longer or shorter version depending on their familiarity with you, the formality of the context, and the time limitations of the conversation. As outlined above, your story should end with a call for support, so that the connector knows what you're asking of them and why you've chosen to speak with them specifically.

After sharing your story and giving the connector an idea of what you're seeking from them, you'll want to turn the conversation over to the connector by asking them to share their advice. Throughout the conversations, don't be afraid to jump in with questions both about the connector's journey to their current role but also about their advice for you. Below are some sample starter questions you might try out. We've broken them down into questions about the connector's experience to open the conversation and questions about your path to ask after you've told your story. Generally, it's helpful to start with the former and end with the latter. Of course, you will have to trust your conversational intuition. If it seems right to move things around, it probably is.

Questions for Your Connector

Questions to elicit information about the connector's experience and knowledge of the field:

- How did you decide on your field and how did you go about pursuing it?
- How else do people get into this field? Where did your peers or colleagues start out?
- What are the fields with which you have the most contact or overlap?
- Where were you in your career at my age and what were the key decisions or challenges you faced at that time?
- What do you wish you had known about the professional world when you were just starting out?

Questions to reality-check your interests:

- What questions do you have about the needs and motivations I've shared?
- How do you feel that these interests line up with what you know about me?
- What additional interests do you think I have that I missed?

Questions to identify job or career options:
- Given what I've told you about me, what sorts of careers or jobs seem to fit my story?
- What have you seen people do who have similar interests to mine?
- What are the obvious things about finding work that I'm likely to overlook because I'm new at this?
- What general career advice do you have for someone in my situation?

Questions about options for gaining hands-on exposure and experience:
- How do you feel that these paths or fields line up with what you know about me?
- If I wanted to get exposure to that field, to try it out, what opportunities might be appropriate?
- What are some low- or modest-commitment jobs or volunteer opportunities that I could try part-time or for a short time? (We discuss these low- or modest commitment jobs—what we call "modest investments"— in detail in the next chapter.)
- What do I need to know about these paths or fields?
- If you were me, how would you find out more about this field/these fields?

Serendipitous Connectors

To gather information about the professional world, Carly asked *a lot* of people they met in everyday life how they decided to do what they do—regardless of what job they had or if it seemed to them like an interesting job.

This shed light on the different ways people decided what to do and the steps they took to get there. It also demonstrated how common it is for people to just "end up" in a career, without ever having really decided to take that route. Asking people how they got where they are can give you an understanding of how a lot of traditional "work your way up" career advancement scenarios really worked. It can also give you the opportunity to hear individual stories of people who are especially entrepreneurial or creative about their approaches for getting into less traditional fields.

Whether you ask your connectors specific questions or gather information less formally, like Carly did, how well you listen to their answers, and how you respond to them are equally crucial to getting the most information and establishing the best possible relationship with the connector.

Listening Well

To ensure that your connector feels that you hear and understand them, and for you to come out of these conversations with as much information and insight as possible, you'll need to listen well. This may seem obvious, but it's easier said than done. There are two key skills for you to practice in your conversations with connectors that correspond directly with good listening: paraphrasing and asking short, open-ended questions.

Paraphrasing

Imagine that you are in an informational interview with a connector and they've just laid out four ways you might be able to meet your interests, or that they've shared a long story about their own career path. Where should you go next with the conversation? How do you make sure you're not missing important details? How can you ask the additional questions you want to ask while also acknowledging what the connector has just said?

Paraphrasing is an essential listening skill that helps you to clarify what is being said and to simultaneously demonstrate that you're taking in and appreciating what someone is telling you. It's simply restating briefly what the other person said, reflecting it back to confirm your understanding and to acknowledge what they said. During conversations with connectors, you can paraphrase at two levels: the level of content and the level of feeling.

Paraphrasing at the Level of Content

This is useful when you're discussing specific details that could be relevant to your career. Your goal is to capture the essence of their statement, and then restate it in a succinct way. A simple method is to repeat back a summary of what you have heard.

> *Example:* So you're saying there's no easy way to get hired in a district attorney's office here without a law degree, but your colleagues in Philadelphia have taken paralegals before. So that might be a better place for me to start. Did I get that right?

By doing this, you give the connector an opportunity to correct you if you've misunderstood, and to elaborate on the point and add more detail.

In addition to helping you clarify content, using paraphrasing to hash out specific details like this can also slow the conversation down and allow you to better digest the information. This provides you with more opportunity to identify points that need further clarification and to come up with questions on the spot, instead of realizing two days later that you have a burning question you wish you'd thought of during the meeting.

Paraphrasing at the Level of Feeling

This involves reflecting back the emotions and feelings a person is expressing as they talk. This is something that many of us do instinctively during conversations with people we know: Your friend is telling you about a super hectic week at work and you respond, "Oh my gosh, so exhausting." It may not seem as natural to do this with a connector you don't know well, but it can be very helpful. Reflecting back someone's feelings addresses our universal desire to be heard and seen. One of the ways that you can make an informal or formal meeting with a connector meet their interests is to ask them about their experience and then genuinely listen and seek to understand it.

At the level of feeling, paraphrasing can be particularly effective when a connector is sharing a personal story rather than listing specific advice directed at you. Instead of focusing on specific details—as you would when paraphrasing at the level of content—here you are seeking to make a brief, general summary about the feelings that you're hearing in the connector's story. For example, a connector might describe the first three chaotic years of getting their startup off the ground. They might communicate some feelings about this experience directly, giving you an opportunity to reflect back.

> *Connector:* "Things were constantly going wrong. I felt like I had to be available 24–7 because people were always calling me to put out their fires."
>
> *You:* "It must have been crazy to have people constantly demanding your time. That sounds so stressful."

It is also important to pay attention to the connector's body language. Chances are, their body language is communicating the same emotions that they are expressing verbally. In the example above, the connector might give a tired sigh when thinking back to those days. Your response lets the connector know that you appreciate, empathize with, and hopefully can learn from their story. This helps build the relationship. If, at the end of a conversation, you and a connector feel like you've made a genuine connection and gotten to know and appreciate each other, even just a little bit, that conversation could be the beginning of a fruitful professional relationship, rather than just a one-off information exchange.

Paraphrasing at the level of feelings can also coax out a more personal, or even intimate, side of their story. Imagine you added a question to the example above: "That must have been so stressful. How did you make it through?" This might prompt the connector to tell you how they rely on daily meditation to keep a clear mind or how invaluable it was to have a supportive group of friends. As a result of this kind of sharing, you and the connector can now delve further into the topic of how to stay sane while starting your own company.

Asking Open-Ended Questions

As we just touched on, when you reflect back what a connector has just said, you also have an opportunity to ask a question. The goal of your question is to open a space for the connector to continue sharing whatever information they think will be most relevant to you. It's likely that at this early stage in your career, you might not know enough to ask specific questions of connectors. Your task at this stage is to take in whatever connectors have to offer, until you've built up enough of a knowledge base to ask more specific, discerning questions—which, for all of us, happened as we began to get clearer about our career directions and moved into Phase 2: Increasing Access. Open-ended questions help the conversation flow smoothly and allow both parties to focus on the heart of the conversation without getting caught up in convoluted questions or awkward silences.

Your manner of asking questions and your conversational style will ultimately depend on your personality. Justin's style tends to be more direct. He finds this very effective in his work as a mediator, and it complements his enthusiastic, outgoing personality.

> *Connector:* I started out in finance and spent a couple of years
> doing the analyst thing, but found that I was unhappy with
> the environment. What got me was how single-minded
> all of my colleagues were. They seemed to be completely
> focused on climbing the ladder within the company at the
> expense of everything else in life.
>
> *Justin* [Paraphrase]: So you wanted to be around people who
> had interests outside of just work? [Open-ended prompt:]
> Could you tell me more about that?
>
> *Connector:* Yeah, that's exactly right. At first, I thought
> all finance jobs were like this. But as I started talking to
> friends, I saw that some of the private wealth management
> people at smaller funds worked just as hard but cared about
> other things besides work . . .

Carly finds that a less direct style fits more comfortably with their personality.

> *Connector:* I loved science, but I knew that lab research wasn't for me. I became a freelance science journalist and also started working in a writing center at the university, coaching engineering students on their writing.
>
> *Carly* [Paraphrase]: So you've really been able to bridge science and communication. I'm trying to figure out how I can do that. What are other things you think I should know if I decide on a similar route?
>
> *Connector:* Start writing. Every day. As soon as possible. My freelance career didn't pick up until I started getting real traffic on my blog.
>
> *Carly* [Open-ended prompt]: I'd love to hear more about how you got your blog going.

Carly and Justin's examples illustrate two distinct ways of communicating. Both approached connectors in the way that was most natural to them, and both led to productive conversations. We encourage you to mold and adapt our advice to fit your language and communication style. While some styles will certainly work better with some connectors than others, what's most important is that you communicate in a way that feels authentic and natural, and helps you listen and respond effectively. No matter what style works best for you, the goal is the same: to confirm your understanding and ask open-ended questions that keep the conversation rolling.

Expressing Gratitude

After meeting with a connector, thank them. This is, of course, simple courtesy, but it also opens the door for an ongoing relationship. As you meet more and more connectors, you develop a robust network of contacts, mentors, and colleagues. And having a strong network is more than just knowing these people. You need to consistently nurture your connections and keep the links alive by staying in touch with the people who have helped you in the past.

Showing your appreciation after a meeting or informational interview is the first step.

Tips on appreciation:

- Be timely—ideally, sending thanks the day after your meeting and certainly within the week.
- Be concise and genuine.
- Reference a specific piece of advice or information that you found helpful. This lets them know that you've absorbed what they said and that you value their input.
- For extra credit, reinforce the conversation with a thoughtful addition: pass along something they'd be interested in—an article, an announcement about an upcoming talk, a relevant funny comic, etc.

Demonstrating your appreciation not only shows your gratitude, it also lets the connector know that you are engaged, conscientious, and reliable. If you show them that you have taken their advice, they are likely to feel that their time spent meeting with you was worthwhile.

You have at least four options for appreciation that you should use liberally: spoken, email, notes or cards, and positive word of mouth.

Spoken

At the end of your conversation, thank the person you spoke to for their helpfulness and generosity with their time. If you can, highlight specifically several ways they were most helpful to you.

Email

Always follow up a meeting, even the most casual conversation, with an email thanking them for their support and insight. Although the email might be as short as a line—"Thank you so much for taking the time to meet with me today!"—it still adds to the conversation. Plus, a thank-you email gives you a good reason to be in touch with them and allows you to add in any follow-up questions or requests you may have. For example:

Dear Amy,

It was great meeting with you today. I am so grateful that you were willing to share your experience in digital and social media marketing with me. I was embarrassingly underinformed about it before our meeting. You've given me a great understanding of the lay of the land.

You mentioned two articles in our conversation that you said you'd be willing to share. One was on marketing to people under the age of 30 and the other was on the structure of a good blog post. If you're still willing to pass those along, I would like to read them.

Thanks again for your time. I hope that our paths cross again soon.

Sincerely, [Signature]

Remember to take notes during meetings if you want to follow up with connectors about specific references or suggestions. It's possible the connector will not remember who else they suggested you meet with or what books and websites they recommended. If you ask them in a general way to recall and forward any sites, information, or contacts they mentioned, this may require an unwelcome effort on their part. Instead, take down the references they make during your conversation and ask for these specific resources. If you make it easy for them, they'll be more likely to respond.

Emails serve a second important purpose: They allow you to stay top-of-mind with connectors. If you do go on and read a book or article they recommended or if you meet with someone they recommended, follow up and let them know. And be judicious about what you send along. Share content that is relevant to your professional connection and that you genuinely think they will find interesting, useful, entertaining, or informative. It's especially meaningful to update a connector about a positive change in your life if their guidance was an important factor in that change. They will be pleased to know that you've put their advice to work. Not many people follow up with connectors in this way; it can help you stand out from others.

Notes/Cards

These add an extra flare to your appreciation. In the age of social media, email, and texting, a hand-written or typed note or card easily sets you apart. Sending a card via snail mail shows that you've gone the extra mile. Use your judgment to decide when a meeting with a connector merits a note or a card. An informal chat on a drive to a conference probably does not merit a thank-you note, but two hours of impromptu coaching over lunch probably would. When in doubt, send a card. People's business addresses can often be found online. If you don't know people's addresses, you can either ask or find a time to hand-deliver the note, which can be a nice excuse for a brief interaction with the connector to keep yourself top-of-mind.

Positive Word-of-Mouth

It can be uncomfortable to receive compliments directly. Words of praise are almost always welcome when they come secondhand, though. What you share about your connectors is likely to make it back to them, so be careful to share the positive with others and think strategically about who is most likely to report back. If someone you've had an informational interview with comes up in conversation with someone else, take the time to share what you authentically admire about them.

Lots of social science research—ranging in focus from business units to successful marriages—highlights the importance of frequent appreciation in the health of relationships. People need to hear more appreciative statements than critical statements to have a healthy relationship. Chances are you aren't going to overdo it.

A Final Note on Sincerity

Inauthentic appreciation can be much more damaging than no appreciation at all. When we're talking about sending gratitude, we're not advocating that you go through some song and dance just to get ahead. We're saying that gratitude and appreciation are essential parts of human connection. As with everything in this book, we feel that meaningful connection, conversation, and thoughtful negotiation around your and others' interests are the keys to more effectively navigating the phases of your career.

3

Putting Your Interests
to the Test

The final ingredient of Phase 1 is exposure—getting firsthand knowledge about the fields or types of work you're leaning toward. There's really no substitute for a reality test. Here we introduce you to negotiating with people who can provide you with opportunities that meet your core Phase 1 interest—finding clarity. The main purpose of these Phase 1 negotiations with decision makers is to gain exposure to different work environments without overcommitting to any single option. Of course, the type and variety of opportunities you'll be able to engage will depend on your personal constraints—finances, family, and so on—but your aim at this stage of the game is to find modest but meaningful commitments, such as a summer internship, shadowing someone while maintaining your day job, or quitting your 9-to-5 to volunteer for several organizations for a couple of months each.

While you are now seeking to test your options, remember that you're still gathering information; you're still figuring out what your work goals really look like. You have two purposes in your negotiations with decision makers in Phase 1: The first is to find opportunities that allow you to deepen your knowledge of how an industry or field works—in other words, to understand its ecosystem. The second is to hone and continually revise your Interest Profile based on real experience.

Your first task is to identify your ideal options as well as the adjacent ones. Ideal options are the ones that seem to fit your interests perfectly. For instance, if you love puzzles, computers, gaming, and working on one project intensively, then an ideal option might be software engineering. Although you should continue to target an ideal fit, don't underestimate the value of exploring adjacent opportunities. These adjacencies may not seem appealing immediately because they're barely on your radar, but don't count them out too soon; they may have the potential to meet many if not all of your current interests. Considering adjacent opportunities in addition to the obvious ones will expand your opportunities for gaining exposure and thereby will help you gain momentum.

When considering potential adjacencies, cast a wide net. It's better to spend time job searching while simultaneously volunteering, shadowing, or working part-time in an adjacent job—all the while honing your skills and meeting potentially valuable contacts—than to spend months and months solely job searching because you're only really looking at "ideal" job opportunities. The more you do, the more you will get in terms of clarity, skills, and concrete networking connections. You never know where the most important lessons will come from or what combination of circumstances and experiences will finally make things click. Consider the examples of Kamal and Leah.

During his Phase 1, Kamal shadowed a pharmaceutical sales representative for a few days and realized that sales just didn't appeal to him. But he was intrigued by the challenge of connecting people to health and medical resources, and this experience nudged him toward his current career in public health policy.

Similarly, Leah dreamed of getting into sports marketing for a professional baseball franchise. A family friend connected her to a two-month marketing internship at a local TV station. It wasn't exactly what she wanted, but the opportunity basically fell into her lap, and it had at least *some* relevance to her dream. In the end it gave her two important things: a window into the world of marketing and, as it turned out, insights into some striking downsides to the world of professional sports, because one of her superiors had worked for a professional team in the past and shared his experience with her. After this short internship, Leah realized that she wanted a glitzier work environment and broader marketing responsibilities than either a sports team or a TV station could offer. She followed her interests and eventually joined a large advertising agency with several professional sports team accounts.

Do you *have* to pursue these adjacent opportunities? It depends. If you find what seems like the perfect opportunity in the form of an all-consuming graduate program or a full-time job, go for it! But here's the tricky part: How can you tell if your "perfect" opportunity really is perfect? At this stage, you can't know what you don't know. Sampling work in areas adjacent to your current target fields will give you the information and experience you need to make a more informed choice about what is the "perfect" opportunity. Furthermore, the seemingly ideal opportunity may simply be unavailable to you. More often than not, adjacent opportunities are the only ones immediately within reach.

Think of it as part of building a foundation. Rather than leaping at your final goal, you are looking to take a solid next step. For now, you don't need to know what the best opportunities for you are, you just have to find experiences that allow you to gain greater clarity about what those ideal opportunities might be.

The key to making this exploratory period work is flexibility— that is, maintaining your availability to pursue diverse and related opportunities. As an illustration, consider Guadalupe.

Guadalupe wants to know if marine biology is truly her passion before she commits to an expensive and time-consuming graduate program. She works part-time as the penguin caretaker at a local aquarium, conducts volunteer research with a local university professor studying the reproductive cycle of sea urchins, and is part of an advocacy group that supports sustainable, local oyster farming. Through these three jobs, she is not just learning about the broader landscape of marine biology, she is also familiarizing herself with diverse facilities and equipment, testing her skills, and getting to know the field's research organizations, associations, and funders. The advantage of this hodgepodge of opportunities is that it gives Guadalupe a broader exposure to the field than taking any single job would have. It will also ground her in the realities of each of these roles in a way that introspection, reading, or even conversations with connectors would not.

Unfortunately, Guadalupe's job at the aquarium is demanding more hours from her. This job is teaching her a lot about caring for marine life, but it doesn't meet her interest of learning about lab research and sustainable farming. Without flexibility, she will have trouble maintaining the other two jobs and thus lose the chance to learn what they have to offer. The aquarium supervisor sets Guadalupe's schedule without any knowledge of her other commitments and often books her to work on days when the professor is doing interesting field research she could participate in. Further, because the aquarium is short staffed, finding a substitute is difficult, and switching shifts with someone else is generally discouraged. All of this means that Guadalupe is missing important learning opportunities with both the oyster farmers and the professor.

We'll pick up Guadalupe's story below and consider how she might have avoided this scheduling problem in the first place.

Staying Flexible . . . for Now

Gaining exposure to a field that interests you will be easier if you have flexibility at the outset. But how do you invest your time and energy in opportunities while maintaining flexibility? Most medical schools have built exposure and flexibility into their third- and fourth-year curricula. During this period, medical students spend between two and six weeks working in rotations in a wide range of specialties. By the time they are applying for residencies, these aspiring doctors will have been exposed to the work environment, lifestyle, and particular challenges of a wide range of medical specialties.

This structure offers students a way to make informed decisions about what field they want to enter *after* being exposed to that field. Whether a medical student applies to residencies in surgery or neurology, they are doing so with a good sense of what they are getting into, thanks to several weeks of experience in that world.

Unless you're a medical student or you're in a similarly structured field, you won't have this kind of built-in exposure to possible career paths in your desired field. Luckily, you don't need a set of built-in rotations. You can create your own program of exposure to different jobs and fields. Your specific approach will vary based on your situation, interests, and the people you know and meet. But the idea is to maximize your exposure to different career paths using whatever connections and opportunities are accessible and affordable to you.

Ask your sister-in-law to let you spend a couple of days helping out at her motorcycle repair shop. See if your neighbor, who does woodworking as a hobby, will let you tag along to a woodworkers' convention. Shadow your uncle at his work for a day; even if his particular job doesn't interest you, you'll still learn something. Apply for summer internships. Volunteer once a week with a local ambulance company, taking EMT training if necessary. Attend a trade show. Sit in on a day of trials at the courthouse to observe the litigation world.

We think of these opportunities as "modest investments" in your career. They probably won't be lucrative, but they won't take up all your time or break the bank either. We're talking about shadowing for a weekend at the vet your dog goes to, not working yourself into the ground to win the country's most prestigious biology internship. We're recommending starting off with a lifeguard certification class, not jumping impulsively into a degree in sports medicine. You can pursue these small opportunities while you're in school, or on evenings and weekends if you're already working. They require little money and a modest investment of time, and they will yield a lot of useful learning.

We suggest that you create for yourself a period of exploration similar to that of medical school rotations. Which modest investments you choose and how much time and energy you commit to them will depend on how well they seem to satisfy your interests, the level of commitment they require, how difficult they are to acquire, and your financial, geographic, and time constraints.

The main reason we are emphasizing flexibility is that the 9-to-5 mindset is still so pervasive that people tend to take for granted that they'll have to commit a predetermined amount of time to a single job. In reality, the time you commit to something, or the way you organize your schedule, is often up for negotiation—especially if you are volunteering, interning, or setting up some kind of informal opportunity.

Some suggestions for modest investments:

Attend conferences, lectures, or industry events. These events offer workshops and presentations about hot or emerging topics, best practices, and who's who, as well as give you a glimpse into the landscape. You'll see how people dress, treat each other, and interact at recreational activities.

Join organizations dedicated to what you want to do. This can include trade or industry groups and activist organizations. You will get a deeper understanding of the field than you would by just attending a single conference.

Take training sessions. Training sessions expose you to the substance of what people do in an industry, help you build concrete skills, and can help you decide if you are truly interested in the type of work or not. You may also be able to get to know the instructor, who could later become a connector or decision maker.

Shadow—accompany and observe people during their work. Shadowing enables you to see behind the curtain. You can get a feel for a "day in the life."

Help decision makers, or others in their organization, when you have time or expertise they lack. You will discover what it is like to work with people in the field and how your skills fit into this field. Consider coauthoring articles with a decision maker, lending technology know-how, providing foreign language skills, helping with administrative tasks like sending emails, or taking notes during meetings. This could also involve doing something a decision maker has wanted to do for a long time but has never had time to do—like creating a filing system or cataloguing their books.

Volunteer or take on a modest internship. Internships and volunteer opportunities can range from formal to informal, structured to unstructured, and from a few weeks to a year. Many individuals and organizations provide flexible, low-intensity internships to newcomers in a field. Sometimes these are advertised internships, although in many cases you can approach a decision maker directly and propose that they take you on as an intern—and negotiate what that would look like. Even when no internship is officially posted. Similarly, some organizations, especially not-for-profit institutions such as hospitals, zoos, crisis hotlines, or schools, provide structured volunteer opportunities that give you hands-on work without requiring a huge time commitment.

Accept a demanding internship or part-time employment. There are few better ways to get a sense of a field's landscape than by working part-time or taking on a more structured, formal, or demanding internship that gives you the chance to do real work in a given field. Of course, such opportunities can range in the amount of time and energy they require, so you'll need to examine whether a given option meets your flexibility interest.

Assist in whatever capacity is relevant in your field. Examples include research assistant, teaching assistant, laboratory assistant, and data entry assistant. There's also cleaning up backstage, giving tours at the planetarium, and helping a small business or sole proprietor.

Try temp work. This offers you the same benefits of part-time employment with a major pro of getting exposure to lots of different fields. The con is that you will have little control over what fields you are exposed to and might work in areas that aren't relevant to your interests.

Freelance, consult, or subcontract. Freelancing and consulting allow you to see what it is like to work with companies and individuals in your target field. You might draw on a distinct skill set you already have to test out a field that's new to you—to get near the work, even if you're not quite doing it yet. For instance, as you're exploring the idea of going into international development, you could freelance for a microcredit organization translating documents from English into Turkish. If you have the relevant skills and experience, you could jump into a freelance or consultant role in international development directly.

As noted in chapter 2, the ideal way to learn about these modest investments—what's out there, where to look, which ones are instructive, which are a waste of time—is through your conversations with connectors.

Combining a few of these different experiences will also require you to manage how you distribute your time among them. In many cases, you can negotiate for flexibility from the outset of an opportunity, rather than getting boxed into an inflexible situation. Tad has a story that illustrates that negotiation.

> *TAD:* After much soul-searching and many discussions with connectors, my nephew set his sights on a full-time job as the IT manager for an international nonprofit organization. He had a solid background for this job, and his interests included making a significant impact on the organization, securing health benefits, traveling, and maximizing his time for other opportunities. Instead of assuming that the job responsibilities and structure were set in stone, he negotiated terms to meet his particular interests. He asked that he have responsibilities for only the North American offices and the autonomy to design IT projects, as well as to work 32 hours Monday through Thursday and have Fridays off. He had originally asked for 40 hours Monday through Thursday, but they could not meet his salary requirements, so they agreed on 32 at a lower salary. The organization accepted his terms because it allowed them to fix and advance their IT with a higher quality candidate than expected.

Making Good Trade-Offs

Of course, flexibility also has its disadvantages. Holding a few part-time opportunities probably doesn't pay as much as a single full-time job, particularly if some of them are internships or volunteering. You may not be eligible for the benefits you would get if you were in a full-time position. Working full-time plus moonlighting or juggling numerous jobs at once can make scheduling a nightmare and make it hard to maintain a healthy work-life balance. Still, trying as many experiences as possible is the best way to figure out what you're good at and interested in. As we said, this period is an investment meant to launch you into better-paying, less hectic, longer-term, and more fulfilling jobs in the future. Being involved in several jobs and organizations also increases the circle of people in your network; it increases your versatility. In Phase 1, Finding Clarity, this gives you many more people to learn from and more future potential collaborators for the next three phases.

The modest investments you pursue will naturally be based on your constraints, and it's important to make sure that any trade-offs you make are genuinely beneficial. If you are willing and able to do some unpaid work, think about whether the opportunity is worth it. Will it address your skills or experience gap? If it pays, but not much, be clear on the decision maker's requirements and expectations. Again, will the opportunity offer exposure that is useful enough to make it worth accepting the compensation they are offering?

Other ways to make it financially possible to spend a stretch of time doing the exploratory work of Phase 1 is to find creative ways to temporarily lower your cost of living or ways to work a low number of hours for a high rate. You will likely be able to free up more time and mental space to get the exposure and training you need if you're able to make some sacrifices in terms of comfort or quality of living. That said, there is no time limit for Phase 1. Don't rule out your ability to explore these types of modest investments—like shadowing or attending an evening training course—even if you have to accrue these experiences one at a time over a period of many months.

There's a good chance your schedule at the end of Phase 1 will be a little chaotic. As long as you can manage, that's a good thing. Still, we want to stress the importance of not letting the chaos of this patchwork of experiences get in the way of your doing excellent work. If you are too tired from your moonlighting job to perform well at your daytime internship, you won't be able to perform your best in either role. In any given job, you want to do good work, impress your superiors, and complete your tasks in an outstanding fashion.

Find ways to go above and beyond so that your superiors will want to help you out. Doing high-quality work that meets the interests of your employer is one of the best ways to garner immediate and future support. If you excel, your employer will be more likely to want to help you with your career exploration and advancement. If the message you are sending is one of being overtired, cutting corners, or not honoring a commitment you've made, then you are not representing your skills and value the way you could be.

Bringing in Decision Makers

When seeking opportunities in Phase 1, you have your interests—gaining exposure while maintaining flexibility, among others—and the decision maker granting or denying you access to an opportunity has theirs. For example, if one of the interests of the clinical coordinator considering hiring you for a per diem nursing position is not needing to micromanage, she will be screening candidates for their ability to work independently and proactively throughout the busy day in the emergency room. If you can show that you are an independent, proactive problem solver, she is more likely to hire you because you will have demonstrated that you meet her interests. Decision makers will involve you in opportunities if they think you'll meet their interests.

When looking for opportunities that provide you flexibility, remember that not all decision makers—especially employers—think about offering flexibility. A well-thought-out presentation of your own needs *and how you can meet your employers' interests* is more likely to win you the flexibility you need in Phase 1 than not asking up front and trying to work around restrictions later. That's what Guadalupe experienced at the aquarium. The basic negotiation know-how you need to do well at this point is twofold. (1) Identify and speak to decision makers' interests. (2) Make a few small adjustments to the story you crafted in the previous chapter so that what you ask for reflects the specific interests you hope to meet through this opportunity. You can achieve both of these in your preparation before negotiating.

Preparation: Your Interests and Theirs

To get the most out of a negotiation and achieve a mutually beneficial arrangement, it is wise to prepare. No serious athlete goes into a competition without practicing. Nor would an attorney represent a client in a trial without careful preparation. Preparation is an acknowledged key to success, and yet a staggering number of people dive into negotiations without preparing at all. Even though at this early stage of your career, your negotiation preparation may be relatively straightforward, it is still important.

The key to these early negotiations with decision makers is to be clear about your interests, and as clear as possible about theirs. You will most likely go into the conversation with only a hazy understanding of their interests, but they will come into clearer focus as you begin to speak with them. To divine their interests before the meeting, you might try to speak with connectors who know them, or gather as much information about them as possible through online research. At this early stage in your career transition, it's okay to make educated guesses about the decision maker's interests while preparing. Below is a set of questions to help you prepare a summary of your interests and theirs.

It helps to sit down and write out answers to these questions because it ensures that you will get more clarity than you would simply pondering them in your mind.

Your interests:

- Which interests of mine am I hoping to meet through this opportunity?
- How much time am I willing to commit to this opportunity, given what I am likely to gain from it?

Their interests:

- What interests does this decision maker have?
- What are they seeking from their employees/volunteers?
- What about my background and skills could be most compelling and relevant to this decision maker?

Now, let's weave the answers you generated into your story.

Revisiting Your Story and Getting Clear on Your Call for Support

Frame your story around your interests and theirs. The better you understand their interests and demonstrate an ability to meet them, the more likely you will be able to meet your interests too. This is what negotiation, at its core, is all about. To appeal to decision makers, your interests must be packaged in a way that they can recognize: If they believe that the opportunity they're providing you is part of your vision or path, they may be more inclined to help you. They want to have a sense of what you stand to gain. You'll be better able to negotiate for your needs and maintain flexibility if the decision maker has a clear sense of your motivations and how you approach the new role you're looking to take on.

In the previous chapter, you built your story to communicate where you are in your career development and asked for a connector's advice on next steps. Here you'll adjust that story for a specific decision maker you will be meeting with soon. Your story will expand a bit to articulate how a given opportunity fits into your overall career aspirations, what flexibility you need, and why you would be a good fit for what that decision maker is looking for.

The outline of your updated story will look something like this.

1. Biographical information
- Provide relevant experience.
- Include how you came across this opportunity (if this is relevant).

2. Passion
- Explain why you want this opportunity.

3. Interests
- Discuss theirs. Test the educated guesses you've made about their interests and ask about what you missed.
- Discuss yours. Yours might include flexibility and exposure.
- Mention elements of your experience that might appeal to this decision maker. What past experiences will show them that you're a good candidate to meet their interests?

4. Constraints
- Briefly mention any relevant constraints that need to be considered in order to meet your interests. At this stage in your career, requiring flexibility is a common constraint.
- Frame your constraints in terms of your interests and what you imagine theirs to be. (See Guadalupe's notes below for an example of framing this way.)

5. Your specific call for support
- At this point, you're asking for a specific opportunity and for specific parameters that would help that opportunity meet your interests.
- While preparing for your negotiation, take the time to consider and write down what you really want to ask for. (See Guadalupe's example below.)
- You may also be asking the decision maker to recommend other modest investments or to connect you to other decision makers.

Returning to Guadalupe's situation for a moment, let's specifically revisit her story to break down how this type of conversation could play out. If she had been thinking about flexibility from the get-go, she might have tried to negotiate for greater autonomy when she first interviewed for the job at the aquarium. How might she have approached that negotiation with the decision maker?

Here is how Guadalupe's preparation notes for her conversation with the aquarium supervisor might have looked like.

Guadalupe's interests:

- Find clarity through exposure to the industry; find out if marine biology is right for me.
- Earn money to cover my expenses.
- Gain professional/career information and contacts.
- Maintain flexibility to pursue other opportunities.
- Be seen as a reliable employee.
- Ensure ease of scheduling.

Aquarium supervisor's interests:

- Health and well-being of the penguins and other marine life
- Competency of staff
- Aquarium visitors are satisfied
- Promoting environmental sustainability through visitor education
- Efficient use of resources/staffing
- Predictable staff coverage
- Ease of scheduling
- Good relationship between management and staff
- Low turnover
- Trustworthy employees

So Guadalupe's story notes might have looked like this.

1. Biographical info

- I minored in marine biology in college, but it's been hard to find any relevant marine biology jobs. I was excited when I saw this opportunity posted on an alumni page.

2. Passion

- I want to do something about the potential extinction of marine species.

- In school, I became fascinated with and concerned about the effects of climate change on marine ecosystems around the globe.
- I plan to learn as much as possible about marine populations in different parts of the world and the effects of global warming on each of them, hence my focus on penguins, sea urchins, and oysters.

3. *Interests*
- I'm considering applying to marine biology PhD programs, but that's a huge commitment, and I want to be sure that this is the right field for me.
- Plus, I want to build skills and experience that I can use in grad school or in future jobs.
- Staff competency and the well-being of the animals: In college, I spent a summer tracking and researching sea turtle breeding patterns. We also cared for injured sea turtles, so I have experience with direct care.
- Visitor satisfaction: I've worked as a server for the past two years, so customer service is important to me. I'd be interested in learning more about how animal caretakers interact with aquarium visitors.
- I can imagine that visitor satisfaction and efficiency in scheduling staff are important to you. What else is important to you?

4. *Constraints* (framed in terms of her interests and theirs)
- Guadalupe's interests/constraints around flexibility: If I apply to grad school, they will expect me to have research experience, so I'm volunteering in a university lab. It's important to me that my schedule at the aquarium lets me spend time at the lab.
- The aquarium's interests/constraints around reliability: At the same time, I'm sure it's important to you to have reliable employees, and I wouldn't want to commit to this job unless I can be the kind of dependable penguin caretaker you need.

5. *Specific ask*
- I'd love to work here. It seems like a great opportunity to explore marine biology.
- As I've shown, and as you will hear from my references, I am reliable, hardworking, and focused on excellent customer experiences. I hope to work out a schedule that is efficient for you and also allows me to keep my volunteer role at the university lab.
- The lab I work for generally does experimental work on weekdays, so I'm hoping to be there about three days a week. If it works for your scheduling needs, I'd prefer to be able to work weekend shifts at the aquarium.
- I'd like to be able to commit to a certain number of hours per week and avoid going over those hours.

Of course, Guadalupe isn't just going to recite this story in one chunk. These details will come out in a back-and-forth conversation. Depending on the context of your meeting with a decision maker, you might not have very much agency to shape the conversation—particularly in more formal interviews, which the interviewer will likely lead. Because the conversation may not unfold as rehearsed, it's important to remember to be adaptable when talking to a decision maker. Being well prepared is the best way to be adaptable. If you've identified your and their interests in advance, and mapped out your story, you will increase the likelihood that you'll be able to adapt and get what you need from your interaction with the decision maker.

Guadalupe has now developed and rehearsed her story and is ready to share it with a decision maker. After they exchange introductions and pleasantries, Guadalupe and the supervisor dive into the details of the penguin caretaker role.

Supervisor: Yes, cleaning the tanks, feeding the penguins, preparing the food. Eventually we'd get you more involved with the visitor education side too. Right now we're looking for someone to work 30 hours a week.

Guadalupe: Overall, the job sounds great, especially the

future involvement with visitor education. Thirty is a few more hours than I was hoping to commit to. The lab where I volunteer usually does their experiments on weekdays. To get into grad school, I need to have some substantial research experience, so I'd been planning to spend three days a week in the lab where I volunteer. I was hoping that you might need someone for weekend shifts. Is that an option?

Supervisor: We don't have any weekend-only positions available. With this position, the schedule changes week to week. Sometimes it could be Monday to Thursday. Other weeks you'd have Thursday through Sunday, which would give you plenty of weekday time in the lab.

Guadalupe: Ah, and it changes every week.

Supervisor: Yes, depending on a variety of factors. Actually, though, there's another option, which is a per diem position. That's basically "as needed." We would call you to fill in, which could be last minute, or it could be planned in advance when other staff members have vacations.

Guadalupe: That sounds like a good possibility.

Supervisor: It pays hourly, and we can't guarantee a set number of hours per week. There might be weeks where no shifts are available. You could also be asked to cover in a different department every now and then, anything from the gift shop to the freshwater exhibits.

At this point in the conversation, Guadalupe has to consider how well this opportunity meets her interests while the decision maker clarifies its scope and limitations. The 30-hour option doesn't provide her with the flexibility to spend three weekdays in the lab. The per diem option would give her lots of flexibility to pick and choose her own schedule. Plus it could provide exposure to other departments and other aspects of the marine biology field. But even considering these factors, it doesn't meet her interest in having a set number of hours, and it's not as financially stable since she can't predict how much work she'll get in a given week.

Guadalupe could weigh her interests and choose either of those options. She could also pass over this opportunity because it's a fairly big investment that might not meet enough of her interests. She may decide that volunteering in the lab and working with the aquaculture activism group will give her the exposure she's looking for and continue waiting tables for income.

Or, she could try to negotiate for a more creative, mutually beneficial arrangement, one that wasn't initially on the table. To do so, she would have to understand more about the supervisor's interests.

Guadalupe: The per diem position definitely sounds like it could be a good option for me. But I'm also curious: When you say that the 30-hour employee schedules depend on a number of factors, what sort of things do you mean?

Supervisor: Well, many things, that's why it changes so often. To start with, it depends how many people we have strictly caring for the penguins and the tanks versus doing visitor education and giving presentations. The aquarium's mission is all about educating people about their oceans, so of course we want visitors to enjoy the presentations and leave with as much information as possible. But it's also my job to make sure that the penguins are healthy. I can't have my employees feeding them late or forgetting to clean the tanks because they're too busy with the education side of things.

Guadalupe: So it sounds like you're really trying to balance those two things—giving visitors a fun educational experience and making sure staff are able to keep up with all of the essential day-to-day tasks.

Supervisor: Exactly. The number of aquarium visitors goes up and down a lot depending on school schedules and weather. During school breaks and nice weather, we're super crowded and need more educators. It's less busy during the school year, but then sometimes we also have big groups of students come in for field trips.

Guadalupe: It sounds pretty unpredictable. I can see why you need employees who are available on all different days. I'm wondering—are the field trips planned in advance?

Supervisor: Yes, the schools are required to make field trip plans weeks or months in advance.

The more Guadalupe talks with the supervisor, the more she will uncover his interests and come to understand how he makes his hiring decisions. For instance, she has learned that he has an interest in balancing the penguins' care with visitor education, and that this can be tough because the visitor volume changes so much. She has also learned that school field trips are one of the big factors that complicate scheduling. If Guadalupe can meet enough of the supervisor's interests, she may be able to negotiate for a different option than the two he originally put forward—an option that better meets her needs. For instance, she might be able to work with the supervisor to come up with an agreement where she commits to 30 hours per week and the supervisor commits to give her mostly Thursday–Sunday shifts, unless he is especially in need of extra weekday staffers for field trips. Because field trips are always planned well in advance, Guadalupe will have at least a month's notice if she's needed on a Monday through Wednesday and can plan her research lab activities accordingly.

In this negotiation, Guadalupe draws on two important skills: (1) preparing for a negotiation by thinking through her own interests and the supervisor's interests, and (2) putting together a compelling story to communicate her needs to the decision maker. These skills allow her to weigh her interests to make a good decision when presented with a set of fixed options—in this case, accept 30 hours, the per diem role, or not accept at all. Further, these skills give her the chance to take a look at those fixed options and, if none of them meet her interests very well, to delve into the decision maker's interests to come up with creative new options that meet both of their needs.

If you're not yet able to distill interests into a creative, mutually beneficial solution, that's okay. If Guadalupe had not pursued a conversation about the supervisor's interests, there would be no possibility of coming up with a third option, but her preparation and her clarity about her own interests would still help her choose wisely between the supervisor's two original options. Many people in Phase 1 aren't yet able to get beyond discussing the fixed opportunities that decision makers present, and that's just fine. You're just beginning to learn this skill, and you may still be early in your career, or at least early in your career change. Your Phase 1 opportunities are meant to be modest investments, after all, and that includes spending a modest amount of energy on your negotiations.

After you spend some time in your own life practicing the tasks of Phase 1, you'll start to notice that you're able to mobilize your expanding negotiation skills to get clarity about your own interests. With that clarity, you'll be able to make informed choices that consider two key interests—maintaining flexibility and broadening your exposure to your interest areas. Dipping your toe into a few fields or a few niches in a particular field in Phase 1 is crucial to being able to take a productive next step in your career. What comes after all this lower-commitment, toe-dipping experience? A target field. Deciding on a target field marks the beginning of Phase 2.

Increasing Access

Conversations with CONNECTORS

4

Committing to a Field

Of the four career phases laid out in this book, we put the most emphasis on Phase 2. This is where you can really set yourself apart. If you commit to the Phase 2 process, based on our experience as coaches we believe that you can achieve a meteoric rise in your chosen field compared to others who skip this phase, rush through it, or don't realize it even exists. We cannot stress enough that the effort you put into Phase 2 is a crucial precursor to that enticing Phase 3 benchmark of doing the work you love in a job that's right for you. Right now, it's all about building up to the point where that job is in reach. It's about access.

With the knowledge, skills, connections, and social or professional capital you build during this phase, you will be ready to leap into Phase 3, Getting Work You Love. Gaining access to that work is more than just contact with the people who make hiring decisions. It starts with your knowledge of the landscape of the field. This includes its points of entry, salient skills, roster of roles and responsibilities, culture and politics, key players and decision makers, how people in the field define success, what they value, and what distinguishes the leaders from others. Your understanding of the landscape—its character and quirks—will help you negotiate a place for yourself in that field.

Of course, the crucial step that comes before understanding and gaining access to *the* field is setting your sights on *a* field. In Phase 1, your goal in negotiating with yourself was to get your broad professional interests clear enough to be able to tell your story to connectors and familiarize yourself with a range of work opportunities that seemed to fit that story. In this first part of Phase 2, you need to zero in on a field that strongly resonates with your interests and fits into your evolving story.

In the last part of Phase 1, Finding Clarity, you engaged in controlled experiments, or reality tests—taking on roles and doing actual work that seemed to fit, either entirely or partially, with your Interest Profile. These modest investments allowed you to make a well-informed choice about what field felt right to you, rather than making a decision based simply on conjecture about what a field or job *might* be like.

Phase 2, Increasing Access, begins with a choice of field, and the foundation for your choice is fit. Gauging fit means taking into account both your gut instinct and a measured analysis. Good decision-making is partly a matter of gut feeling—you just know that this field makes sense for you. And thanks to the effort you put into your modest investments, you have some compelling firsthand exposure to inform your intuition.

Good decision-making also means weighing the information and advice you received from your sources, for instance, from your connectors, from friends and family, from aptitude and personality tests, from economic forecasts, and so on. Your gut feelings should be supported by this external input. A well-fitting career path should feel right *and* make good financial and personal sense.

Because decision-making is deeply personal, we do not prescribe a particular method for arriving at this sort of decision. But we do advise that you make a choice! You are ready to move into Phase 2 when you've found a field that feels *right enough* to both your head and your heart that you want to dive in and explore it. It's hard to feel completely sure about such a big decision, and it's natural to have some misgivings. Rather than getting overly caught up in the big picture—wondering whether a given field is truly the field of your dreams or something you'd be satisfied doing for the rest of your life—the question we like to pose when our coaching clients are considering Phase 2 is, "Does it feel worthwhile enough to completely throw yourself into discovering and exploring this field for the foreseeable future?" Once you've gotten a sense of a field, you can, of course, always step back and decide your path lies elsewhere. But to really reap the advantages of Phase 2, to successfully build the access capital that will propel you into Phases 3, Getting Work You Love, and Phase 4, Building Greater Fulfillment, you need to *fully commit* to this process of discovering a field's nuances, navigating its politics, and evaluating whether it's truly a fit for you.

Everyone's moment of transition from the uncertainty of Phase 1 to the certainty of Phase 2 will look different. Here, to provide a few examples of what it might look like when someone realizes that they're certain enough to dive into Phase 2, we share how the three of us arrived at deciding on our respective fields.

> *TAD:* I had been running a boutique marketing consulting firm, but had started looking for jobs that better met my interests. My primary interests were (1) doing what I considered more important and rewarding work, (2) joining a small firm in whatever new field that would be, (3) working with a team, (4) becoming a recognized expert, and (5) working directly with the end user.
>
> As part of my Phase 1, I met with an industrial psychologist, talked with family and friends, took the Myers-Briggs personality test, and studied the typical career choices for someone with my personality type. I ultimately identified mediation, training, and writing a book as my top options. I was stunned because these were such a departure from my experience in marketing, airline pricing, and hotel management. I didn't know what kind of skills I was supposed to teach or what to write a book about. So I took a basic mediation training and was totally hooked— mediation/negotiation was the direction for me.

During my Phase 2, I volunteered in the Massachusetts district court system for about a year, mediated about eighty-five cases, and started working part-time at a conflict resolution firm. I was building up my access to the mediation/negotiation world while still running my marketing firm. With a foot in both fields, and getting busier, I had to make a choice. I reviewed and revised my Interest Profile, left marketing, and committed myself to a complete transition to mediation, negotiation, and conflict resolution.

JUSTIN: My Phase 1 started by accident right after high school when a friend talked me into trying to run an international NGO supporting young environmentalists. I left this experience with the desire to know way more about the philosophical underpinnings of our economic system, which is what I ended up studying in college. For my senior thesis I worked with a community outside of Philadelphia measuring their ecological footprint and exploring options for helping them become more sustainable. Both of these experiences debunked my assumption that the solutions to our environmental problems are solely technical. I came to see that the interpersonal and political challenges to environmental sustainability were as important as the technical ones. I had taken a mediation class in college, and I was becoming clear at a gut level that being a mediator and facilitator of negotiations rather than an environmental activist was the path I wanted to pursue. With that clarity, I moved to Boston—the epicenter of the conflict resolution field—and began my Phase 2, trying to break into the field.

CARLY: On the surface, my path through Phase 1 looked and felt pretty chaotic. I bounced all over the place. I raised baby lobsters at an aquarium, taught HIV prevention, and worked as an administrative assistant. I gave swimming lessons to kids, went to Bangladesh for a fish farming project, and worked as a cashier. I was a research assistant in cross-cultural psychology and ran after-school programs for teens at a youth center. Despite the chaos, however, there was some method behind the madness. These jobs let me test out whether I wanted to be a research scientist or a science journalist—two options I had seriously considered. They also provided an opportunity to judge whether I should work in public health, international development, or cross-cultural consulting.

Each time I struck one of these options off the list, I was disheartened to feel that I still hadn't found a direction worth investing in. But each time I narrowed my options, I was getting a little less lost. I was learning that the jobs I enjoyed most were people-centered human services roles, like teaching HIV prevention and running youth programs. As I shared in my story in the book's opening chapter, I eventually found my way into mediation—a job I'd never heard of before—by chatting with a customer at the café where I worked.

Finding mediation was a satisfying step, but even that eventually still proved to be part of my Phase 1 journey. I liked conflict resolution, but my gut instinct told me this wasn't a good fit. Mediation was too focused on quick, concrete solutions rather than long-term exploration and healing. The field of conflict resolution didn't meet one of my primary interests: working intensely one-on-one with people to delve deeper into their personal stories and struggles. After conducting many informational interviews, I started to realize that clinical social work met my interests better, and so I dove headfirst into my Phase 2: figuring out how to become a clinical social worker.

Our paths were all shaped by elements of chance, as well as periods of deliberate, thoughtful negotiations with ourselves. The field of conflict resolution, which for Justin and Tad provided a comfortable sense of rightness was, for Carly, just an adjacency that functioned as a stepping-stone into social work. Tad took a single mediation class and was immediately hooked. Carly never had a light bulb moment, but slowly realized over the course of a year that being a therapist could provide the things that felt missing in mediation. We all had occasional feelings of ambivalence and fears of failure, but eventually we found something that felt *right enough* that we could stop our toe-dipping and dive in.

Trouble Making a Decision?

Some people will experience that aha moment, and their paths will become clear. For others, finding a path will be a gradual process. You will know there's still something missing if you have trouble getting excited about your choice and if the idea of a career in that field leaves you feeling restricted.

If you're feeling this way, reflect on your motivations for moving forward. Are you feeling that you have to move forward whether you have clarity or not? Would moving ahead with Phase 2 really give you the progress you're looking for? If you have serious reservations—serious, mind you, not the slight, perfectly natural kind—about committing to the field you've chosen to pursue in Phase 2, you may need to regroup and spend more time in Phase 1. This doesn't necessarily imply starting from scratch. What is important is that you pinpoint what is missing and what is holding you back. Perhaps you need to explore different modest investments to test out adjacent fields. Maybe you need to engage a new set of connectors to refresh your outlook and get new ideas. Or perhaps your Interest Profile will help you identify the problem. When you return to it now, does it reflect your current interests?

Often, feeling stuck moving into Phase 2 comes from a dissonance between the interests you named in Phase 1 and the ones that actually drive you. For instance, you might care deeply about security and avoiding physical risk and only wish that you were a daredevil rather than actually being one. You might wish to be a first-rate number cruncher because you have a knack for numbers, but what actually brings you alive is engaging with people. Just because you're good at something doesn't mean you have to make it your career. Society and our families and friends attach more prestige and respect to some paths than others, so sometimes we find ourselves latching onto interests and values that we would like to be our own, but that don't honestly work for us in practice.

If you retrace your steps in Phase 1 and still cannot pinpoint why you can't come up with a satisfying choice of field to pursue, you may be held back by fears of the unknown, of risk, of taking a leap. If this is the case, seek out a friend or loved one to talk it over with, or a professional coach or therapist to help you deal with what's holding you back. Chances are, if you have taken the initiative to pick up this book, you are thoughtfully approaching your career choices. If you are failing to make progress, it's probably because you've run up against a barrier that you can't overcome alone, which is why it is so crucial to involve other people in your process. In the long run, asking for help will make the difference between ending up frustrated or fulfilled.

Caveats aside, we generally encourage you to just go for it! Even if the field doesn't seem absolutely perfect, give it a shot if you see real potential there. If you get moving into a field and do the work of Phase 2, you will learn a lot about that field. You may end up learning that it's not for you. That's okay. There's a great deal of value you can take away from a thorough engagement with Phase 2 even if you end up changing course later. For example, Tad, as you know, dove into Phase 2 and established a rewarding career as a mediator and trainer in conflict resolution. After more than eight years, he realized it was the deep one-on-one work that he loved the most, so he pivoted to career coaching and consulting. He still relies heavily on the skills he learned as a mediator and as a coach.

When you first enter Phase 2, you likely won't understand the field well enough to know what specific role or job within your field is ideal for you. You might start doing awesome fundraising work that gets you really fired up, but in an organization whose values clash with your own. Or maybe you spend nine months working as a paralegal, doing informational interviews with environmental lawyers and taking the LSAT, and after all that have a light bulb conversation with a connector who helps you realize that your interests are actually pointing you toward environmental engineering. Negotiating with yourself in Phase 2 entails making a choice about what field you want to explore and then getting the most from that choice by learning and adjusting as you go. The beauty of Phase 2 is that you have the freedom to make and learn from decisions that are less than perfect in the short run.

Phase 2 leaves room for these sorts of small moves and realizations, and this mindset of exploring and adjusting is essential to your overall success. Psychologist Daniel Stern and his team call this process microregulation. Each of your small steps forward "perform almost constant course corrections that act to redirect, repair, test, probe, or verify the direction of the interactive flow towards goal."* In that quote they're discussing how infants negotiate interactions with their parents, but their comments are relevant to any improvisational, interactive process, including the career-building process we're advocating.

For example, as Carly mentioned above, they spent about five years jumping around between various jobs and fields.

> *CARLY:* Some of these jobs hardly seemed related at the time, but looking back, each of these "local goals" added up to an excellent foundation for clinical social work, even though I didn't always know that's where I was headed. Running after-school programs for adolescents taught me a lot about building community. Working internationally helped me learn to build relationships with people very different from me. My mediation experience has been

---

* Daniel N. Stern et al., "Non-Interpretive Mechanisms in Psychoanalytic Therapy: The 'Something More' Than Interpretation," *International Journal of Psychoanalysis* 79 (1998): 903–21.

invaluable for doing family therapy. Working in public policy mediation gave me important background for understanding the policies and systems I have to navigate with my clients.

During that five-year period of switching jobs, I often felt pretty lost. The only thing I could do was try to let my Interest Profile guide me. The work and training decisions I made nudged me this way and that—and, in the end, onto a path that has made me very happy. And, now that I can look back on it, my path makes sense and fits together in a way that it didn't always seem to at the time.

With each bit of clarity you gain, you adapt and make shifts to your path and your potential place within the field. The next two chapters will give you a framework that will allow you to make these necessary adjustments and course corrections toward roles, areas, and communities that are the best fit for you.

Defining Access Capital

Even as you make these adjustments you will be acquiring access capital in the form of relationships, skills, reputation, credentials, and an understanding of the inner workings of your field. This access capital is what will allow you to get in the room with the people who make hiring decisions and to be a compelling candidate for them.

What grants you access capital will depend on the field you are seeking to enter. Often it includes your reputation within the field, what people believe about the quality of your work, how well known you are, your concrete skills, your ability to create opportunities, and how many people will vouch for and support you. For some fields, access capital includes credentialing and certification. In others it's all about visibility and public acclaim. Sometimes it relies heavily on relationships.

Your best route to acquiring access capital is to expand your connector base and conduct informational interviews. In chapter 5, "The Art of the Connector Conversation," you'll negotiate with connectors to learn what constitutes access capital in your field of choice and how to acquire it. In chapter 6, "Getting a Foothold in the Field," you will start building your access capital through your negotiations with decision makers.

Committing . . .
to Not Yet Committing

The exploration process of Phase 2 requires committing to *not yet committing to permanent placements*. At this important stage of your job hunt, we recommend that you maintain the mindset of an investigative journalist. Cultivating journalistic distance will save you from prematurely committing to a random entry-level job. If you don't take the time to understand the landscape of your field, then you're likely to waste energy trying to get jobs that aren't a good fit. Or you might go about your job search in a way that simply doesn't work in that particular field and consistently come up empty. Or you might take the first seemingly interesting opportunity that comes along, only to discover that it's a dead end. Basically, we're encouraging you to focus on understanding and acquiring access capital rather than focusing on landing your dream job right away. Take the time to investigate:

- What the field values: the essential or advantageous skills and know-how that will help you access the field and access what you'll need to learn to advance within it.
- Roles that make up the field: its entry-level jobs all the way up to its highest placements. What are the hierarchies and power structures?
- Key players and decision makers: who are the established icons and who are the rising stars and game changers? Who is a potential mentor for you?
- The character of the field: its internal culture and politics—for instance, how success and leadership are defined, the values promoted and discouraged, current

controversies, what the typical work environments are like, and expectations surrounding work-life balance.

Different industries tend to foster unique ways of thinking and behaving. To figure out if this field is a good fit for you, and to eventually be successful within it, you will have to work to discover its mindsets and attitudes, to gain a level of cultural fluency. In some work environments, junior employees are given immediate autonomy and independence. Others can be much more hierarchical, with lower-level employees expected to have all of their work checked by a supervisor. Some workplaces routinely sanction unethical practices, like firing a woman who is pregnant, while other industries expect all employees to prioritize family over work. If you are oblivious to these implicit rules within a field, you are vulnerable to making serious lapses in judgment as you try to gain access.

Self-Care on This Sometimes Bumpy Ride

Your Phase 2 process may get uncomfortable at times. As you try to find your footing and gain access to your chosen field, you may have lingering doubts. Everyone has different levels of tolerance for risk and uncertainty, and it's important to be aware of your comfort level with risk. While part of taking a bold approach to career development means pushing to expand your comfort zone, we encourage you to approach Phase 2 in a way that feels authentic to your personality and to be realistic about your life circumstances.

Since coping with this uncertainty can be draining at times, take measures to support and care for yourself more than you normally might. Now is the time to be intentional about self-care, even when it feels like you are too busy for it. This also means knowing what self-care looks like for you and what is realistic given your financial and time constraints. How do you best recharge your emotional batteries and replenish your motivation? It looks different for everyone. Is it giving yourself permission to go out salsa dancing or to take a long run when you feel pressured to spend every minute job hunting? Or is it giving yourself permission after a frustrating day to eat loads of chocolate and call up a good friend who will be glad to be there for you and let you vent when you're about to give up and resign yourself to your dead-end job or go back to résumé-spamming the internet?

As we emphasize throughout this book, career development is all about relationships and interacting with people. Continually engaging with connectors and decision makers throughout this process ensures that you won't have to struggle alone. Not every connector you meet will be helpful or kind. But some of your interactions with connectors will reignite your confidence. Other interactions will be comforting and reassuring. Still others will spark ideas that will change your life. With enough patience and dedication, your engagement with connectors in the next chapter will inevitably spark new ideas, open new doors, and ultimately pave the way to doing work you love.

5

The Art of the Connector Conversation

Informational interviews are common practice in today's economy, and many career guides claim they are a must. Even so, they tend to offer very little direction on *how* to go about this conversational research: *how* to find people to speak with, *how* to convince them to take time to meet with you, *how* to simply and effectively manage the actual conversation, and *how* to follow up in such a way that you open the door for an ongoing relationship. Doing informational interviews well takes preparation, practice, and a thoughtful approach focused on interests.

Meeting with connectors is a central part of each phase of our approach, but the informational interviews in Phase 2 are especially important. They allow you to gather nuanced, insider information that can be uncovered only by talking with people who are already working in your desired field. What's more, these meetings will likely play a key role in your advancement in the field, both through the information you acquire and the relationships you build through them. Informational interviews—connector conversations—are your best tool for understanding and developing the access capital that will carry you into Phases 3 and 4.

By "informational interview" we mean any conversation you arrange for the purpose of (1) learning about someone's professional experience and job knowledge, and (2) getting their advice about paths and projects relevant to your story. We aren't talking about the common ruse of asking for an informational interview while secretly hoping the connector will give you a job. This ploy wastes a tremendous opportunity to make the most of what informational interviews really have to offer: crucial information and access capital.

By and large, these will be formally scheduled meetings you've requested where the other person specifically sets aside time for you. Sometimes you can also take the opportunity to steer spontaneous meetings—such as chancing upon someone at lunch or at a conference—into an informational interview.

The exchange between you and your connector in these meetings will very often generate creative ideas and unanticipated opportunities that you never would have discovered on your own. Through informational interviews, you will meet people who can help you make course corrections, refine your path, and avoid pitfalls so that you end up clearer about your goals. Informational interviews have the potential to generate future professional opportunities, further contacts, and ongoing mentoring or collaborative relationships.

At the outset of Phase 2, your informational interviews will focus on learning about the landscape of your chosen field—its roles and duties, who the decision makers are, what "success" means in the field, how to develop a strong reputation, what skills or credentials are required for advancement, and who else you should contact. When possible, you should also be looking to gain insight into the interests of specific decision makers whom you hope to work for in the near future—the people who might be interviewing and hiring you later on in Phase 2 and beyond. As you progress through Phase 2 and start getting a better understanding of this landscape and your niches within it, your interviews will begin to focus more and more on learning how to get your foot in the door for specific opportunities—particular jobs, learning opportunities, or other forms of professional development. Going forward, the approach you learn in this chapter for negotiating with connectors will be directly relevant to your negotiations with all decision makers in the future.

Casting a Wide Net

Who can help you identify the path to fulfilling your career interests? This is a tough one, especially if you don't know anyone actually doing the work you want to be doing.

Justin used his grandfather's favorite expression to help him figure out how to proceed: "Do something—anything—even if it's wrong." The wisdom behind this statement is that it's easier to adjust your course once you're already moving than it is to get started in the first place. This is how Justin describes his process when he was looking to gain access to the field of mediation.

> *JUSTIN:* I knew I needed to figure out how to get access capital in the mediation world, but I didn't know any mediators, so I just started doing informational interviews with people I did know. I started with my parents, friends, and former teachers because they were accessible to me. A few of the interviews were irrelevant and unhelpful. Most were off topic. Still, they did lead me to people who were a little closer to what I needed. One of my parents referred to a past colleague of theirs who worked at a divinity school, and she happened to be married to someone who ran a mediation program. It was through him that a whole world of connectors opened up.
>
> The great thing about the informational interview process is that it's self-correcting. I could have started out speaking to circus clowns, and eventually I would have made my way to interviewing with highly experienced mediators. It just might have taken longer. The key to making the process self-correcting is to ask the people you interview what they would do if they were in your shoes, and to be ready to accurately describe what your shoes are like—your situation, interests, and where you're trying to go.

Informational interviews get easier the more you do them. If you start off with folks who are receptive and friendly, you'll have an opportunity to practice, build confidence, and get familiar with the routine and rhythm of these conversations. This includes the necessary advance preparation, informal (but important) small talk, typical questions, and ways of keeping the discussion on topic. In particular, you need to hone your informational interviewing skills and know your stuff before approaching "big fish" connectors and decision makers. These are the people at the top of your field—people who have the opportunity to hire you or connect you to job opportunities in the future, and who have the ability to significantly strengthen or damage your reputation. Be aware that even the people you meet very early in your career might become important decision makers for you later on. Be mindful of the impression you make and of the reputation you're creating for yourself.

Of course, not every person you contact will have done exactly what you want to do, *and* have insightful advice to offer, *and* be willing to take the time to help you think through career strategies. You don't need to get all of your answers in one place—that's why you speak to as many people as possible! Here are some criteria for evaluating potential contacts. People who meet even one of these criteria can be helpful connectors.

- Have they already done and succeeded at what you want to do?
- Do they have a lot of contacts in the field and the ability to point you to other helpful people to talk to?
- Are they a potential ally—someone who will advocate for you by giving your name to other people and speaking highly of your abilities? An ally can also be someone at your level who may not have opportunities to give but who you can collaborate with to share and generate future opportunities.
- Do they have unique insights into your areas of interest or your social identities that will help you clarify what you want to do and how to get there?
- Are they sympathetic and willing to take the time to think through your career questions with you?

- Are they struggling with similar career questions or challenges?
- Are they experienced, insightful, or worldly? Even if someone like this isn't directly connected to your field of interest, they may still have good ideas about how you can forge your path.

Now where do you actually find these people? Here are some ideas about ways to start looking.

- Within your existing network, either professional or personal. Chances are that a few people already in your network know people who can help.
  - Ask friends or family for their stories: "Would you be willing to take a walk with me and talk about how you ended up [doing what you do professionally] and let me bounce some ideas off you about what I'm thinking?"
  - Ask to be connected to additional people: "I am looking for ideas about how to move forward in my career. Do you have any suggestions of people who might be willing to speak with me, given my interest in [your chosen field or core focus]?"
- At your internship, volunteer engagement, or job, especially if you arrange structured meetings with others in your organization. You will, of course, learn from just being around them from day to day, but you'll learn a lot more from setting up purpose-driven meetings.
  - "What would really round out my internship would be 30 minutes to hear about your own path into this field and any advice you may have for me. Would you be willing to meet?"
- By joining academic, trade, or professional organizations and attending conferences and lectures in areas that interest you. Better yet, volunteer to help organize and manage a conference or event.

- Listen for people's stories or ask them about their professional experience as you print flyers or work on the agenda for a conference together. If it is within your means, offer to buy them a cup of coffee or lunch if they will share their story with you.
- Go to classes, training workshops, or lectures where the instructor is someone you'd like to meet. This can be expensive, but if you choose your classes wisely, you'll not only learn from the classroom material, you'll also have insider access to the instructor as a paying member of their class. Ask the instructor if you can contact them afterward to set up a time to get coffee and talk about their path. Keep an eye out for places that offer scholarships or reduced fees for their classes and workshops.

- Through other connectors. In each of your informational interviews, you can ask your connectors who else they think you should meet with. This will give you access to other influential connectors and make it possible for this process to become self-correcting: out of all their contacts, your connectors will refer you to the people who are the best match for your interests.
- By cold-calling or cold-emailing people you've heard about, found in books, or found online. In the case of cold contacts, etiquette and timing can be especially important. We cover this in the next section, "Getting Their Ear."
  - Try to be as accommodating as you can: "May I meet you at your office to speak for 20 minutes about what you've learned about managing your own career path?"
  - Sometimes a person just doesn't have the time or bandwidth to let a stranger "pick their brain" for free, often because they work in an underpaid field, but they still want to help. More and more, people

are offering paid consultations, mentorship sessions, or short online classes that can be well worth the modest financial investment.

Our overall message here is to cast a wide net. During Phase 1, Finding Clarity, you were trying to get breadth of exposure to different paths and fields. Now you've targeted a field and you're asking connectors, "How do you think I should go about approaching this field?" Seek to hear as many connectors' stories and advice as possible.

Not all connectors are the same. We encourage you to keep the following contact hierarchy in mind.

LEGENDS

INDUSTRY LEADERS

ORGANIZATIONAL LEADERS

ESTABLISHED PROFESSIONALS IN THE FIELD

NEW OR ENTRY-LEVEL PROFESSIONALS IN THE FIELD

PEERS AND OTHERS WHO, LIKE YOU, ARE SEEKING TO ENTER THE FIELD

FAMILY/FRIENDS/MENTORS WITH KNOWLEDGE OF OR EXPERIENCE IN THE FIELD

The closer you get to industry leaders and legends, the more formal your meetings tend to become and the higher the stakes tend to get. These connectors have status and influence and are generally harder to access. With this graphic, we're not suggesting that you need to hit every level of the pyramid. Rather, we're saying that the more skilled at conducting informational interviews you become, the more we encourage you to go for the biggest fish you can catch. How? By continuing to ask every connector, "Who else do you think I should meet with?" Or target specific big fish you've heard about and whose work and reputations you admire. Continually scan your network for anyone who might know someone who knows the big fish, and be bold in requesting an introduction, even if you might need to go through a few degrees of connection to get there.

Getting Their Ear

One of the most common misconceptions about informational interviews is that the prospective interviewer is asking for a favor—for advice, guidance, and time—without offering anything in return. This mindset can make it very difficult to pursue them.

But if you view the informational interview as a negotiation, then it's more approachable and carries much higher value potential. Rather than imagining yourself having to ask for a favor, which can be intimidating, you'll be asking yourself, "How do I get what I need in a way that meets the connector's interests as well?"

Yes, it's true that in a normal informational interview, the information is mostly—though not entirely, we hope—flowing from the connector to you. But that doesn't mean the connector doesn't have interests that you can meet in return.

We've talked to hundreds of connectors in recent years and acted as connectors ourselves for scores of job hunters who have approached us for guidance and a glimpse into the inner workings of our respective fields. In our experience, although individual connectors' interests vary, there are certain interests that are common to nearly all connectors, regardless of their field. Try to put yourself in the connector's shoes and consider what interests of theirs you might be able to meet, such as:

- Recognition: being valued as an expert, a respected professional, and a mentor
- Convenience: having their schedule accommodated (and therefore respected)
- Insight: providing the opportunity to learn from you and your unique newcomer's perspective on the field

- Impact: sending a newcomer off in the right direction and knowing that their advice is helping shape your career
- Utility: meeting a potential collaborator or employee who could fit their staffing needs in the future
- Affiliation: enjoying the opportunity to have an engaging interaction with an interesting and perhaps like-minded individual
- Appreciation: having their time, attention, and wisdom acknowledged
- Information: learning about something new happening in the field or at another organization that they know little or nothing about, or just catching up on industry gossip

Some of these connector interests are practically universal human interests, and of course there are overlaps between them. You should be looking to engage some if not all of these interests by showing gratitude in your emails, by deferring to the connector's needs around time and place, and by presenting yourself as a prepared, thoughtful person.

Of course, you don't want to take a one-size-fits-all approach. Interests are specific to the person, and you should try to uncover as much as you can about the connector's interests by doing your homework online—at the very least, reading their bio—and speaking in advance with people who know the connector. What do you know about this person and what's important to them? For instance, some people truly enjoy mentoring for mentoring's sake, while others don't find it particularly gratifying. Does your connector have a reputation for mentoring newcomers and helping them network? Depending on the nature of their job, some connectors don't often interact with colleagues in their field or adjacent fields. They may genuinely welcome the opportunity to learn from you or hear updates about other people in their field whom you've already contacted, as Carly discovered in some of their Phase 2 informational interviews.

CARLY: When I was working in the conflict resolution field and considering switching careers into mental health, a lot of the psychotherapists I met for informational interviews genuinely welcomed the chance to learn from me about dispute resolution and mediation. These topics pertain to psychotherapy, but the professional paths of mediators and therapists don't often cross. I was happy to find myself adding something of value to those conversations.

Point being, don't sell yourself short and underestimate the value of fulfilling these types of relational or intangible interests for connectors. Thinking of informational interviews as occasions to meet the connector's interests can also help allay your concern that your requests for informational interviews will come off as presumptuous or entitled.

CARLY: When I worked as a communications coordinator at a nonprofit organization, I constantly received emails from people who wanted informational interviews with our senior staff members. It was amazing how many of these emailers just assumed that they could waltz in and have an informational interview with anyone at any time. The emails often said things like: "I've read your website and I'm extremely interested in your work. I am writing to set up a meeting with Dan about the possibility of working in this field," or "I will be in town on Tuesday the 10th and Wednesday the 11th. Please let me know which day you could meet."

The emails we received varied from polite to brusque, but even the polite ones often read more like demands than requests. By not demonstrating an understanding that our staff was extremely busy, these emailers neither showed respect for our staff's time and responsibilities nor expressed advance gratitude for the potential opportunity to learn from our staff. Furthermore, in demanding short-notice informational interviews, they revealed their off-putting ignorance of the landscape of our field, where it's common for people's schedules to fill up months in advance. In short, they completely failed to speak to our staff's interests.

To avoid all of these potential pitfalls, we've listed some useful guidelines for requesting an informational interview, followed by a suggested structure and a sample email. We generally make these requests over email, and so we focus on written requests here, but most of these guidelines apply similarly to a phone or in-person request.

Tone and Content

Although we're big proponents of casual career talks with relatives and serendipitous chats with professors, sometimes you'll need to go out of your way to formally request an informational interview from someone you don't know well, or at all. You're more likely to get a favorable response if you project an appealing first impression, and you can do so by focusing on both the tone and the content of your request.

- Write in a way that does not assume they will say yes. You're *asking*, so your phrasing should make clear that the meeting is conditional on their response: "If you're interested, would you have any availability the week of the 8th?"
- Show gratitude and let them know you'd value their input: "I'd appreciate the chance to ask you a few questions about your professional background and the field."
- If they don't know you, include a brief, engaging description of who you are and why you're interested in meeting them. Don't give them your life story; give three or four sentences, maximum. In particular, mention topics or experiences that you both value and have in common.

- If you've met them before or someone has introduced the two of you, remind them of this; they may have forgotten. Do this early—at the beginning of the email or even in the subject line if it seems appropriate.
- Offer to be of service to them in a small way that indicates you understand their needs. If appropriate and within your means, offer to buy them coffee or lunch. Or offer to help clean up after an event, stuff envelopes, or print flyers.
- Use your knowledge of a given connector or your general understanding of the field or the industry landscape to speak to their other interests. If status is especially important to them, perhaps use a deferential tone or include some honest and gently flattering statements. If you know that they're concerned with leaving a positive legacy, let them know that their advice will help you positively influence the future of the field.

Logistics

When you request an informational interview, the other person is most likely to say yes if you can speak to their interests. You might not know all of their interests, especially if they're a stranger, but pretty much everyone has an interest in life being simple, easy, and logistically uncomplicated. You can meet some of your connector's interests by deferring to their arrangements wherever possible and smoothing out any logistical wrinkles in advance.

- Think about their schedule in the context of their job, their field, family situation, and so on. Be sensitive to when they're likely to be free, and explicitly work to propose times around their scheduling needs.
- Always make it clear that you defer to their schedule, and offer to meet wherever is convenient *for them*, even if this means less convenience for you. If it's impossible for you to get to them, then ask if they'll be in your area on other

business; don't assume that they'll travel solely to meet you.

- Make sure you nail down the specifics before the meeting: the time (accounting for time zone differences); the location; whether or not meals are involved; phone/video versus in person; if by phone or video, who will be initiating the call, and at what number or on what platform.
- Show up early! Take the extra time to prepare yourself for the conversation. If they also show up early, then you may get more time with the connector. In case of factors beyond your control, it's helpful to exchange phone numbers, such as for any last-minute delays.
- During the meeting, take notes—handwritten notes so that a device doesn't create a barrier between you and the other person. In addition to helping you remember all the important details afterward, this will also demonstrate to the connector that you are taking the meeting seriously. We don't encourage recording informational interviews because recording can be off-putting, which would compromise your goals of encouraging a candid and frank conversation and building a positive relationship with the connector.

Structure: Bringing It All Together

Taking into account the tone, content, and logistical guidelines above, the following examples are meant to help you structure the specific pieces of your message when you first reach out to each new connector.

1. Your introduction: Provide any relevant context that lets them see a connection or affiliation.

Hi [Connector's Name],

My name is Agatha Wilson. I had the privilege of attending your keynote speech at the IECS conference last week in Santa Monica.

2. Your connection, if applicable: Provide a point of connection between yourself and someone they know and, ideally, respect.

At the conference, I had the chance to talk with Aisha Douyan. She spoke highly of you and recommended that I reach out . . .

3. Your purpose for reaching out: Describe what inspired you to reach out.

. . . because of my interest in environmental engineering.

4. Your ask: Make clear what your specific request is.

If you would be willing, I would gladly buy you lunch sometime in the next couple of weeks to hear about your experience working on your new book.

5. Background information, if necessary: If the person knows nothing about you or if the person who made the introduction is not a close connection, include some information about yourself—not more than three or four sentences.

I graduated from architecture school in Arkansas two years ago and have been working for a small design firm in California since graduation. I had the chance to hear Peter Kazuo talk about permaculture and natural building two years ago and was fascinated by its potential to change industrial norms. I have read many of your articles and would very much like to meet with you in person.

Proposed time and mode of meeting: Give some options for when you could meet while still demonstrating flexibility.

If you'd be willing to meet, please let me know when would be convenient for you. If it's helpful, below are a few times during the next two weeks that would work for me.

March 3, anytime after 3:00 p.m.

March 6, between 9:00 a.m. and 11:00 a.m.

March 7, at noon for lunch

Closing: End the communication by expressing gratitude for their time.

Thank you so much for considering my request. I hope we have the opportunity to connect.

Sincerely, Agatha

Having considered what you can bring to an informational interview and how to approach a connector with a request, let's move on to how you can best prepare for, conduct, and follow up on your interviews.

The Connector Conversation in Two Questions

When the three of us started doing informational interviews, we didn't really think of them as such. We just realized, each in our own way and on our own timeline, that it was essential to have in-depth conversations with other people to help guide our career decisions. Yet, as soon as these conversations are called "informational interviews," they can start to sound intimidating. In our experience as career coaches, we have found that people often feel anxious about their first few informational interviews, and because of this, many people try to avoid doing them. It's an understandable reaction. The word "interview" has a lot of uncomfortable associations! But when you boil it all down, an informational interview is simply a conversation with a connector. Sure, it's a more thoughtful, purpose-driven conversation than your everyday chat, but it really isn't very different from something you've done a thousand times before.

With this in mind, we offer a straightforward approach that is relevant for every informational interview. You ask your connector two essential questions: (1) about their story, so you can learn vicariously from their career journey, and (2) about what they would do if they were in your shoes, so you can hear their advice about your specific career goals.

The key is preparation: taking time in advance to clarify your purpose for the interview. Research consistently shows that negotiators who have a clear idea of what they want to accomplish in a negotiation are far more likely to satisfy their interests than those without a clear goal in mind. Informational interviews are no different. Before the conversation with your connector, think through what the ideal outcome of this conversation would be. It can be tempting to think that the ideal outcome is a job offer. But not only is that unlikely because it isn't the purpose of an *informational* interview, in Phase 2, your objective is to explore what jobs best suit your interests. Again, what you're actually after is (1) a deeper understanding of the landscape and (2) access to people, skills, and opportunities. Your goal should be framed around access capital.

Once you've clarified your overall objective, spend some time preparing for the two parts of your informational interview.

Preparation

Before meeting with a connector, learn what you can about them online, through other connectors, or by reading things they've written. You'll want to find out what they look like, too, in case you ride up in the elevator together or they hold the door for you as you enter the building. Have they written a book or noteworthy blog? Are they involved in any high-profile projects or initiatives that you should be aware of? In particular, look for points of connection and commonality between you.

One of the best ways to start an informational interview on a positive note is by being able to spend time chatting about things you have in common. Are your backgrounds similar in any way? Do you have any of the same hobbies or personal interests? Finally, think about what it is that you most admire about this person. Have you already learned something from their example? Are you seeking to emulate their path?

Make a list of questions you'd especially like this connector to answer about their own experience. Consider what unique, specific information about the field this connector might have. Have they held jobs that are similar to ones on your radar? Did they make a transition from a field you also have experience in? Do they champion a particular cause? Is there a well-known anecdote about them that you want to know more about? Do they have insight into particular educational or training paths? If they share a particular identity with you, such as gender, race, or class, how does this identity affect their experience of working in a particular field? Who else might they recommend you speak with? The answers to your questions may come up when they tell their professional story. If some of the information you know you want doesn't happen to come up when your connector tells their story, you'll be ready to ask them for this information in your follow-up questions.

Next, think about how you want to begin the interview. What small talk might help the conversation get off to a good start? How do you want to ask them to share their story? We share several examples on the next page.

To prepare for the second part of the conversation where you ask what they would do if they were in your shoes, review the story you put together in Phase 1. You'll want to revise this story and tweak it for your Phase 2 connectors, keeping in mind that at this point your goal is gaining access capital. What aspects of your story will help this connector better understand your interests, where you're coming from, and where you hope to end up? Succinctly note relevant points of your story that will help the connector tailor their advice to your specific situation.

Get clear on specific forms of access capital you hope to gain from each connector. This will define your calls for support. Are you trying to understand the ladder of advancement in the banking industry? Do you want to know what a union representative's day-to-day work life looks like? Are you interested in starting a housing co-op but need help understanding local regulations? The more clearly you can explain to your connector the needs you have, the more easily they'll be able to put themselves in your shoes and help you.

Having prepared, it's time to meet with the connector. Below are details for conducting the two parts of the meeting.

Question 1:
Asking about Their Professional Journey

Any number of similar opening questions will get your meeting started:

- Could you tell me about your professional path and background?
- How did you get into this field? Into your current role?
- I really admire your work on [a project]. How did you decide to do this work?
- I'm especially curious about [a particular piece of their résumé]. How did you find that opportunity and what did it lead to?

Your aim is to ask an open-ended question that will get your connector talking—and ideally get them excited to share their story with you. Asking about the connector's path is a good way to find a window into their experience, wisdom, past mistakes, and thought process. With any luck, your connector will leave you with knowledge (or at least good clues!) about the landscape of your field—a bit about its history, players, and politics—and how to develop access capital within that world.

Let them tell their story, with as little interruption as possible. They shouldn't feel like they're being interrogated. Besides, we find that most people have a lot to say about how they got to where they are, so a hands-off approach generally works. If needed, letting the connector know what you admire or appreciate about their work, or mentioning which parts of their story most interest you, are two ways to help them focus on what you most want to hear. If a connector seems willing to share but is giving very limited details, then it's up to you to take a more hands-on approach and ask questions that will encourage them to delve deeper into their story.

As your connector is starting to wrap up their story, or if they turn the conversation over to you—for instance, by asking what else you'd like to know—be sure to ask for more details if you suspect there's more for you to learn.

Question 2: Asking What They Would Do

Tell the connector a bit about where you are and where you're trying to go, and ask them how they would try to get there if they were in your shoes. This is where the story you crafted during Phase 1 comes back into play. You have to give a succinct and accurate picture of where you are and what's important to you, so that they will be able to (1) give advice that's relevant to you, (2) help you get the information and contacts you need, and (3) help you change course if you're not quite heading in the best direction yet.

When you ask a connector to put themselves in your shoes, you're asking them—albeit in a casual, off-the-cuff way—to invest in your professional development, even if only for the duration of your meeting. You're opening the door for more empathic, impassioned advice that comes directly from the connector's unique perspective. This is what makes informational interviews so powerful.

You can read about the benefits of getting an MBA online, and any businessperson can give you some generic thoughts on the pros and cons of going to business school. But only a connector who has heard your story and interests can tell you, "You know, with your experience in the public sector, you should look at this joint MBA and MS in forestry management they have at the University of Endor. It's not the most famous program, but it has everything you're looking for." Only a connector can speak to you about their path to becoming an illustrator and then finish the conversation with a moment of brilliant personalized direction: "My niece works for a magazine aimed at the transgender community, and she's always looking for gender-nonconforming illustrators. They can't pay as much as some of the big publications, but they do pay their artists, and it would be a great way to start getting your work published!"

If your specific questions don't get answered during steps 1 and 2, you can raise them toward the end of the interview. Also, if this doesn't come up on its own in your interview, be sure to ask for suggestions of other relevant people you could interview and if there are any particular skills or experiences your connector thinks you should be looking to acquire in the near term.

Managing the Flow of the Conversation

Over time, you'll naturally find yourself getting savvier about the questions you ask and better at managing these conversations. One of the simplest ways to facilitate a smooth informational interview is to be transparent about the two questions you'll be asking: "I'd love to hear the story of your career path, share a little bit about my goals, and then discuss any suggestions you might have on how I could meet these goals. Would that be okay with you?"

By revealing your approach, you're laying out an agenda for the meeting so that both you and the connector have a general idea where the conversation will go. If you have other specific questions you'd like to discuss during the meeting, you can also give a heads-up about these as you set an agenda: "I also have a few questions about graduate programs that I'd like to ask you as we go along." These additional questions may be about any part of their background or experience that is relevant to you. Clarifying time expectations should also be part of the agenda-setting process at the beginning of the meeting. Even if you suggested a time frame for the meeting in advance, the beginning of the meeting is a good time to confirm how long your connector is able to meet. Be ready to wrap up at the agreed-upon time.

If you're someone who is able to process information on the spot easily, you'll be more effective at redirecting the conversation to the topics you'd most like to discuss and at asking relevant follow-up questions. If it's not your strong suit, that's not the end of the world. You simply need to be aware of your conversational style and abilities and to approach the informational interview in a way that suits you. If you find it difficult to process everything you're hearing in the moment, come prepared with more questions written out in advance so that you don't have to come up with as many questions on the spot. And take as many notes as you need so you can think through the information later.

In the end, the success of an informational interview isn't only about your style of approach. There's no accounting for chemistry. Sometimes you'll find that you have an easy connection with the other person and that the conversation just naturally flows. Other times you won't click so easily, the conversation will be somewhat labored, and you'll need to work harder to carry the conversation forward. It's inevitable that you'll have conversations of both sorts. But exchanges of both types can be equally informative, so don't be disheartened by the talks that require more effort.

During the interview, if you find that you've learned everything you came to learn and the conversation isn't flowing naturally, you can gracefully draw the interview to a close by saying, "Well, those are all the specific questions I had for you. I really appreciate you taking the time to speak with me. Is there anything else you think I should know about before we close?" This might give the connector a new angle of conversation to follow for a while, or, if they don't have anything else to add, then you can thank them again and exit with pleasantries and some small talk if that seems welcome.

Following Up

After an informational interview, always send a thank-you. Your follow-up can be as important as the informational interview itself. (For a review of the importance of thanking connectors and tips for doing so, see chapter 2, "Expressing Gratitude" on page 78. A strong email or handwritten thank-you note can meet a connector's need for appreciation, and it demonstrates that you are thoughtful and reliable. A follow-up note or email also serves to remind the connector about your meeting, making it much more likely that they will follow up on any offers they made to link you to other contacts, opportunities, or resources.

Overcoming Hesitations about Informational Interviews

Even people who profess to like the idea of informational interviews often avoid actually doing them. Why? These interviews can be daunting for any number of reasons. Perhaps you're among the many who are fearful that connectors won't want to speak with you or that you'll feel like you're wasting their time. Maybe you're hesitant to ask strangers for guidance or you're worried you'll appear ignorant or indecisive. You might be reluctant to let people know you're thinking about a job or career change. In almost all cases, the benefits of informational interviews are worth the stresses and risks. But with the two fundamental informational interview questions in hand and good advance preparation, you'll be in great shape to make the most of these meetings.

If you find that you consistently avoid doing informational interviews, you might need backup. Ask a friend to sit with you while you draft and send initial emails to connectors, and have your friend call you a few days later to make sure you're following up with those connectors. Hire a career coach if that's in your budget. Have a relative run through a mock informational interview with you. If the prospect of asking people about informational interviews gives you a sense of vulnerability and you are struggling to take the risk, we recommend two resources from Brené Brown that have been helpful to our clients, and to us: her TEDxHouston talk, "The Power of Vulnerability" and her book *Daring Greatly*.*

---

* Brené Brown, "The Power of Vulnerability," June 1, 2010, https://brenebrown.com /videos/ted-talk-the-power-of-vulnerability/ and *Daring Greatly: How the Courage to Be Vulnerable Transforms the Way We Live, Love, Parent and Lead* (New York: Avery, 2012).

It may help to remember that informational interviews are, first and foremost, interactions with other people. They are largely about connecting over shared interests and passions, and sharing stories—and it's a two-way street, from expert to novice *and* vice versa. While we believe that approaching informational interviews as negotiations leads to valuable strategic thinking and the fulfillment of mutual interests, at their core, these interviews are about making good human connections, from setup to follow-up. And this means that they allow for flexibility in process and improvisations in content. What's most important here is to meet and talk with people about career development, in whatever way works best for you.

6

Getting a Foothold in the Field

Once you've devoted enough time and effort to meeting with Phase 2 connectors, you will have a much better sense of who's who and what's what in your chosen field, and you'll have loads of ideas for how to develop your access capital. Your next step is to approach decision makers who can grant you access to people, skills, and experiences that will make you a qualified and desired applicant for the kinds of jobs you want down the road.

What's the difference between connectors and decision makers? Connectors primarily connect you to information and to other people who have additional information. Decision makers are the gatekeepers who can grant you access to opportunities, experiences, and skills. For example, when you sit down for coffee with a friend of a friend to ask what it's like to be a high school teacher, you're speaking to a connector. When you go to a job fair and offer your résumé to the representative at the Teach for America booth, you're interacting with a decision maker. The difference lies mainly in what *you're* hoping to get from the interaction: information versus access to a concrete opportunity.

Decision makers hold the keys to all sorts of opportunities, not just jobs. Depending on what kind of access capital is necessary to advance in your particular field, you might find yourself seeking a variety of skills and opportunities in Phase 2: Maybe a personal trainer certification course. The opportunity to co-teach a class. A commercial driver's license. A research assistantship. The chance to collaborate on a project with a more experienced artist.

Phase 2 is often a winding road. Maybe you're applying to a graduate program in Mesoamerican archaeology that requires you to be fluent in Spanish, but your Spanish is rusty at best. Your room-mate's brother, Eduardo, teaches advanced Spanish at the commu-nity center, and he's looking for a volunteer teaching assistant. If he takes you on, you'll get to improve your Spanish without paying the hefty tuition for the class. Eduardo doesn't have any connection to archaeology, but he's an important Phase 2 decision maker for you because he can grant you access to an essential skill–building opportunity. You're likely to find yourself negotiating with decision makers who you'd never anticipated meeting and who don't seem to have a direct connection to your overall career goals. Yet, like Edu-ardo, these folks can help you gain the access capital you'll need to advance in your chosen field. It's a series of helpful twists and turns like this, which no one could have concretely laid out in advance, that take you through Phase 2.

Again, at this point, you're not aiming to get the job that loves you back just yet; your aim is to strengthen your profile as an attrac-tive candidate for the job market in your field—to become a poten-tial asset to the field and its established players. All of this will build your access capital by improving your reputation, strengthen-ing your skills and abilities, and sparking connections. This doesn't necessarily mean taking on a conventional entry-level job in your desired field, since that might overly constrain your time and nar-row your focus. It's helpful to remain flexible at this stage because it's likely you have skill and access gaps that no single job can fill.

So what are your options for building access aside from getting a full-time job in your field? To answer this, first we must look at what actually builds your access. When approaching decision mak-ers at this point, you are hoping to land roles and participate in activities that will help you:

- Get consistent access to this or other decision makers who have opportunities that interest you.
- Develop the skills that are valued and sought after by the relevant decision makers.
- Become credible as a professional within the field.
- Develop a reputation as someone who is responsible and does high-quality work.

In chapter 3, "Putting Your Interests to the Test," you made modest investments to get exposure by testing out fields that intrigued you. Now you'll use modest investments to build your access to decision makers and prepare yourself for the Phase 3 goal of getting work that you truly love. Look back at chapter 3 (pages 88–90) for an in-depth discussion of possible modest investments. Many of those same suggestions apply here too, only now you're privileging opportunities that build your access capital in your chosen field rather than opportunities that maximize your exposure to many different fields. For instance, attending a conference will put you in the same room as decision makers who might be hiring interns or freelance workers. If you take a training workshop, you can spend some time at breaks or meals getting to know the trainers, one of whom might allow you to shadow at their office for a week, or hire you to do some background research for a future course they're designing. If you do a project, intern, or work part-time for a decision maker, not only will you have access to them, but they will see how you work and you can schedule time to talk with them specifically about your goals and career path.

Someone you first met as a connector might become a decision maker at a later point in your career. Likewise, someone you'd thought might be decision maker could end up being a connector. For example, let's say you set up a meeting with a research scientist who recently posted an opening for a new lab assistant, anticipating that you would be speaking to a decision maker. During the conversation, though, you find out that she has already filled the position. But she recommends several articles you weren't aware of that are currently revolutionizing the field and suggests getting familiar with this cutting-edge research because it will help guide your job search. In the end, she turned out to be a connector instead of a decision maker, and that's helpful too.

It may turn out that it's worth going for a full-time placement at this point because the access granted by this job is so incredible that it outweighs the lack of flexibility. When you investigate specific opportunities, which we discuss in the next section, remember that your focus is now on how you can interact with and prove yourself to decision makers.

Of course, the options available to you will inevitably depend on your specific circumstances, such as the field you're entering, the decision makers you might engage, and the amount of time and resources you have at your disposal. You might need to do your Phase 2 explorations on top of your existing 9-to-5, using your lunch breaks to hold informational interviews or taking an hour here and there to shadow people in your prospective field. Or you might be in school, working part-time and doing internships. Here are a couple of examples from our own experiences to help give you a better sense of the kinds of things you can do to advance into your chosen field, prior to landing a great long-term job.

During Justin's Phase 2 informational interviews, he learned from one connector that a senior practitioner at a local conflict resolution organization, let's call her Julia, was a key decision maker in the field. As one of his Phase 2 goals, Justin set out to find a way to be in the same room with Julia on a regular basis.

> *JUSTIN:* With the help of one of my connectors—a colleague of Julia's— I was able to set up a meeting to explore ways I could support Julia's work. My interest was just that broad—to spend time around her in any way she found useful. As it turned out, she was working on several projects that required research, note-taking, and an extra set of hands for conducting a few trainings. Over the next three months, I helped out occasionally on an as-needed basis. I wrote meeting summaries, ran microphones at events, did

background research for large-scale facilitations, and helped edit a Wikipedia page. Doing these tasks, I learned what decision makers value in an entry-level employee. I got to sit in on staff meetings and see what senior practitioners were working on and thinking about. By working alongside Julia—at events, client engagements, or at her office—I was able to meet other practitioners in the field whom I would not have had access to otherwise.

None of this work was what I ultimately wanted to do. But I wasn't looking to get the ideal job at this point—I didn't have enough access capital to get the kind of job I wanted yet. At this point, I was seeking an opportunity to build a relationship with an established leader. And, through Julia, I was seeking access to modest investment experiences that would help me build my skills and gain a deeper understanding of how the field of conflict resolution worked.

During Carly's first few months of researching the mental health field, they attended a lecture and worked up the courage to ask one of the presenters for an informational interview. This single informational interview led to a surprising amount of access capital.

CARLY: I learned a lot about this connector's day-to-day work as a psychotherapist, and she clearly and succinctly communicated the pros and cons of working in such an emotionally demanding profession, which was essential information for me about the landscape of the field. She introduced me to a particular area of theory and research that I've since fallen in love with and which ended up really influencing my educational choices. She also pointed me in the direction of a modest investment job. I had previously thought I was too inexperienced to get a job in mental health, but this connector suggested that I apply for entry-level work at two specific places.

Thanks to her encouragement, I did, and got hired at a well-known psychiatric hospital. It was a low-paying, part-time job that I squeezed in alongside my existing part-time job as an administrative assistant. I only worked at the hospital about 16 hours a week, but these hours were instrumental in building my access capital in the mental health field. I got hands-on experience developing clinical skills, and I filled some knowledge gaps. The prestigious name of the hospital lent credibility to my later applications for graduate school. Through the colleagues I met there, I started to develop a relevant professional network, and so on.

That should give you an idea of what you're looking for when approaching decision makers in Phase 2. Now let's talk strategy about how you make those opportunities happen.

Approaching Decision Makers with "Yesable" Proposals

Because you are very likely starting out as an unknown to any of the decision makers in the field, your approach has to be strategic. You simultaneously have to get the decision maker's attention, make a good impression, and find a way to persuade them to give you an opportunity. If you are successful on all three fronts, you will not only gain access to an opportunity for skill development and better understanding the field, but you'll also be top of mind with the decision maker when they're hiring.

One of the most effective ways to achieve these three goals is to approach decision makers with what we call "yesable" proposals.* A yesable proposal is exactly what it sounds like: a proposal that invites a "Yes!" in response.

In essence, a yesable proposal puts forward a plan that (1) is well formed and framed in terms of the decision maker's interests,

---

* The concept of a yesable proposition is from Roger Fisher and William Ury's *Getting to Yes: Negotiating Agreement without Giving In* (New York: Penguin, 1991), 79.

thus making it easy for them to say yes, and (2) leaves space for the decision maker to negotiate the details: You are proposing an opportunity that you believe would be of benefit to both parties, one the decision maker might accept without any alteration but is also open to amendments, should the decision maker wish to make any.

You could be the most competent candidate in the world, but if the decision maker can't see the connection between hiring you and getting their interests met, they will not make you an offer. Again, as we mentioned in chapter 5, your best route for learning about a decision maker's interests before you meet them is by speaking with your connectors.

Crafting Yesable Proposals

It's important to put together yesable proposals rather than simply stating what you want for many reasons.

- People are more likely to help you meet your needs if they can see how doing so will meet their own.
- Decision makers tend to be busy people. If you leave it entirely up to them to come up with a way for you to help or get involved (by asking only, "What can I do to help you?"), they may just say no to your offer of help, even if they might actually appreciate it, because they don't have the time or bandwidth to think up something for you do.
- Yesable proposals allow you to advocate for yourself without being overly pushy or entitled. You're making a genuine effort to put together an option that is good for them, and you're putting their needs at the forefront of the conversation.

Of course, preparation is essential for crafting compelling yesable proposals. The connectors you've developed relationships with will be able to assist you in identifying what the decision maker's interests are or what they're likely to be. Without at least an educated guess about your decision maker's interests, your attempt to engage with them here and in later phases is far less likely to be taken seriously, much less accepted.

To illustrate how good preparation leads to successful yesable proposals, and to show what a yesable proposal might look like, we'll take you through Angela's bid to get involved in a documentary film project.

Angela is an aspiring film producer with a degree in journalism and a minor in film, and she is seeking to get a foothold in the world of documentary film production. She could definitely use some onsite shoot experience, and she needs to learn about the studio system, the festival circuit, funding and distribution channels, and a whole host of other aspects of film production. Through a series of informational interviews, Angela discovered that a small production company that has produced a set of documentaries on gold mining is about to start a project on a region in Peru that is facing an impending influx of multinational mining corporations. She'd be overjoyed to work on this project at any level of production, and she's been able to secure a meeting with the production company's executive director, thanks in large part to an industry connection she made during her Phase 2 informational interviews. Her challenge now is to figure out what kind of proposal she could pitch to the executive director that would meet his needs and convince him that she is right for this project.

Through another of those informational interviews—this one with a film school instructor who was familiar with the executive director's work—she learned at least this much: that the executive director sees himself as a mentor to young talent, and that he is personally invested in the social and environmental impacts of international mining practices, particularly in South America, where his family is from.

So Angela knows a couple of the executive director's broader personal interests. But what about his project-specific interests? What does—or might—the project need right now? She makes a short list of likely possibilities based on her knowledge of the field:

- Logistical support on the ground in Peru
- Spanish-speaking editors to help with story editing and subtitling
- Access to funding
- Publicity for the movie, including promotion at film festivals

Beyond this, Angela needs to consider how she fits into the picture. What contribution could she make to the project, and how can she present this to the executive director?

- She is passionate about film as a platform for exploring problems and advocating in support of important work done by nonprofits. (The environmental impact of mining has not been an area of special interest for her, but she is definitely behind the broader purpose of this documentary.)
- She cares about social justice and preserving marginalized and indigenous cultures.
- She is proficient in Spanish, but isn't familiar with Peruvian slang or the accent, nor with the local indigenous languages.
- She is American, but her father is from Argentina and has a history of activism in the region. She may be able to set up further connections between the production company and nonprofits in that region, as well as help to get the film screened in South America.

From this prep session, Angela comes up with the following proposals:

1. She could go to Peru to help the field team with logistics, such as booking hotels or flights, setting up interviews, or arranging for ground transportation. She could do minimal translation work for non–Spanish speaking members of the film crew and be available for general support. To make this feasible, Angela would need the company to cover some of her expenses, including travel and food. Angela is confident that she can find someone

through her network of connections to put her up for free or, failing that, she could try couch surfing, and so she is willing to leave the cost of accommodations out of her proposal. Also, because she knows how to stretch a food budget and is able to buy food at the local markets, she's willing to take the cost of food out of the proposal if necessary.

2. Without going to Peru, she could help on the project doing first-round editing and subtitling, which could save time for the fluent Spanish speakers on staff who would only have to go back and make corrections rather than subtitle from scratch. She could offer to do a trial subtitling of some early footage to demonstrate that it would be a back-end time saver. In return, Angela would ask to sit in on the US meetings of the production team to learn about their process and have the chance to ask individual members questions.

3. Angela could be taken on as an assistant to the producer, helping the producer with basic logistics and to liaise with the directors and editors. If there were room in the project for this ideal role, Angela would happily offer her services—either for pay, if the company is not tight on cash or, probably more valuable for her, in exchange for mentorship from the producer. And hopefully from the executive director as well. Her interest here is getting direct access to the action and decision-making that gets serious documentary film projects off the ground.

Armed with her draft proposals, Angela can then dig further to discover more of the decision maker's interests during the negotiation (an aspect of the proposal conversation we delve into a little further on) and use what she learns to finalize the most compelling proposal on the spot. Before Angela can share her ultimate proposal, she first has to engage the decision maker. From there she will formulate her proposal based on the interests that she hears during their conversation.

Turning to Angela's upcoming meeting with the executive director, compare the examples below of how Angela might approach the actual conversation with the executive director and make an effective, yesable proposal. For each scenario, her first attempt represents an approach that job hunters often take. Her second attempt is based on our coaching.

Offer Concrete Ways to Meet Their Interests

Typical approach: I am really interested in doing work for your company. I think the work you do is amazing, and I want to be a part of it. I am interested in doing production work on documentary film projects that tackle social and environmental justice issues. Your mining documentary is an obvious fit for me. Is there somewhere I could help with the Peru film project?

In moments of stress and busyness, asking a question that requires someone to make choices and come up with creative ideas often feels like additional work that person is being asked to do. Unless the ED just happened to have something concrete in mind right before Angela walked in, he probably would respond with something like, "Thank you for your interest. I'll be in touch," which, as many of us know from experience, rarely leads to anything. This dynamic appears in social situations as well: When a friend is facing a crisis, we often say, "Please let me know if there is anything I can do." Our friends often thank us for offering but don't actually take us up on the offer, even though they probably really could use the help if they weren't too overwhelmed to come up with ideas for ways we could help. If, though, you ask your friend, "Can I bring you dinner one night this week so you won't have to worry about cooking?" they're much more likely to accept. Yesable proposals operate under the same principle.

Coached approach: I've heard about your Peru gold mining documentary project, and it sounds fascinating. If there were a way I could help your team, I'd love to be involved. I imagine that this kind of project would need logistical and organizational support in Peru, and support from Spanish speakers to do subtitling and promotion. I'm hoping that we can find a way for me to help out that would make sense for you. I've heard that you are dedicated to the development of newcomers in the film world, and I know this would be a valuable experience for me. Would you be willing to take a few moments to consider how I might be able to contribute to the project?

In the coached approach, Angela started a conversation and piqued the ED's curiosity by identifying some of his potential interests, as well as listing a few concrete areas where she may be able to help.

Respect the Decision Maker's Autonomy, and Don't Get Positional

Typical approach: I think you should take me on as the ground staff person to organize your logistics.

Coached approach: I took some time to think through how I might be able to help and wanted to share my ideas with you. For one, if you need on-the-ground logistics and administrative support, I would be willing to relocate to Peru for three months to help get the project set up. I could handle hotel reservations and flights, set up interviews with local residents, figure out where to get replacement equipment if something breaks, and so on. In order to make that work financially, I would ask to have my flights and food covered. I'm confident that I can find a place to stay during my time there.

A second option I considered was helping with subtitling on the interviews you already recorded. I speak Spanish and thought I could take a first crack at the translations into English for the subtitles, and then whoever

normally does your subtitles could just clean up my work
rather than starting from scratch. I'd be happy to do a
test run for a short stretch of dialogue to see whether your
editors would find this useful.

  With both of these ideas, my aim is to be around your
team and learn from your process and the great work you
do. At this stage in my career, I am most interested in being
compensated for my work through mentorship and chances
to learn through observation. This could look like allowing
me to be a fly on the wall for meetings of the production
team, or having a monthly lunch meeting where I ask you
more about the industry. Does any of this sound like it
could meet your needs? If not, is there another arrangement
you'd propose?

In the first example, Angela took a positional approach, making a single, narrow suggestion—almost a demand. After coaching,
Angela advanced the needs of the ED first while fitting them in
with her own. Even if she doesn't perfectly understand his interests
yet, she likely has some of them right and made it clear that she's
considering his situation. She asked him if she got his interests right
and how he might tweak the plan to make it a better fit. She was
specific enough for the executive director to have a good idea of a
potential plan, and she gave him room to adapt it. Her proposal was
clear and direct, while respecting the executive director's authority.

Show That You're Aware of Industry Conventions, Even If You Seek to Break Them

Typical approach: I'd like to be a production assistant.
Coached approach: Obviously, I would be thrilled to join
  you as a production assistant. I realize that would be a bit
  unorthodox since production assistants usually come out of
  a newsroom internship or have editing and script-writing
  experience. Still, if you'd consider me for this or some other
  role, I know I'd be able to do high-quality work for you,

and I think my eagerness to learn and flexibility around travel and compensation would make me a good fit. If not, I would gladly volunteer to do runner work for the project here in the US for the next month to give you a sense of what I'm like to work with.

In the first—a typical job-hunting example—Angela asked for something unusual without any respect for or acknowledgment of convention. This can come off as entitled or oblivious. In the coached scenario, she demonstrated her sensitivity to the field and a respect for its conventions while at the same time making a case for why she wanted to disrupt convention. If it worked out, she would get an opportunity she wouldn't normally be able to get with her level of experience. Plus, she also gave the ED the option of setting up a volunteer trial period so he could make a more informed decision about whether to hire her after he'd seen her work.

When it comes to breaking convention, people have different responses depending on their personality, industry culture, and other factors. Some decision makers admire the initiative of those who seek to dive right in the deep end, while others see that as disrespectful. Again, your connectors can probably help you anticipate how a particular decision maker might respond to any attempts to subvert convention.

In each of the three scenarios above, the coached proposal is more yesable because, rather than an open-ended offer to "do anything," the proposal actively addresses specific needs of the decision maker. To respond to the yesable proposal, the decision maker has to expend far less mental effort imagining how you might be able to meet their interests because you have already laid that out for them. The more information you have about the decision maker's interests, the better this kind of prepared proposal can work.

Even if you do have a good idea of what the decision maker's interests are, it is always wise to ask and confirm your understanding. Sometimes this comes before you make your proposal, and sometimes afterward—it depends on the situation, the patience and available time of the decision maker, and how much information you have going in.

Be sure not to box yourself in with assumptions. When Tad was looking for a job in the hotel business in Boston earlier in his career, he landed a meeting through a connection with the regional vice president of a chain that had recently lost its regional pricing director. Tad had a strong background in pricing and the job had not been posted yet, so he was feeling very confident.

> **TAD:** I approached the interview as if I was applying for the job of pricing director—a post I assumed they wanted to fill. I jumped right in and sold myself as a pricer and nothing else—I was perfect for this imagined job opening! After I was finished with my speech about why I'd make a great pricer, the vice president looked at me and said, "That's very interesting, but we have decided not to fill the open regional pricing role. It will all be handled out of the home office in the Midwest. We have other regional placements available, but it is very clear that you're focused on pricing. Thank you for coming in." If only I had asked the interviewer about his interests first. I would have had a chance to talk about how I could have fit with the needs of the company. Whoops.

In situations where you have minimal information about the decision maker's interests in advance, it's okay to start an interaction with open-ended questions about their interests rather than putting forward options based on little or no information. Once you learn their interests during that meeting, you can work with them in the moment to figure out some options that could meet their interests. Sometimes you can use a combination of tactics, for example, drafting some yesable proposals before the meeting and then tailoring those drafts during the meeting, either in your head or by having a brainstorming conversation with the decision maker about what they think might work.

One of Justin's Phase 2 decision makers, let's call him Jay, was a respected professor at a local university. Justin was interested in working with and learning from Jay—but he wasn't sure how that would happen. He didn't know enough about Jay's interests to put together a yesable proposal until after their first meeting.

> *JUSTIN:* During the meeting, I asked open-ended questions to explore Jay's interests and get a sense of how I might be useful. As it turned out, I was lucky with my timing. Jay had been mulling over how he could evaluate student perceptions of a clinical negotiation program he ran at his university. He was just getting started on this evaluation project and seemed open to letting me assist. After the meeting, I emailed and asked in an open-ended way how I could help him with the evaluation. I received no response.
>
> Instead of waiting indefinitely or resending my original inquiry, I drafted a concrete proposal. Based on what I now knew about the program, I suggested conducting a set of interviews with students over a three-month period, as well as sending an online survey to alumni of the program. I proposed that Jay and I meet once a month and that I check in about my progress once every two weeks with one of the other professors involved in the project. I had a hunch that this wasn't Jay's top priority and that other responsibilities kept getting in the way. The fact that I was able to provide a detailed and sensible plan saved him the effort. With a few tweaks, Jay accepted my plan and I started conducting evaluation interviews shortly thereafter.

Delivering Yesable Proposals

To preparing the content of your yesable proposals, it's crucial that you put some thought into how you're going to deliver the proposal and manage the conversation.

In order to have the chance to deliver a yesable proposal, you first have to gain access to the decision maker for long enough to make your proposal. The best way to do this will depend largely on circumstance. Generally, the more face-to-face contact you've had with a decision maker, the more likely it is that they'll meet with you, and the easier it will be to get your proposal accepted. Getting access to Phase 2 decision makers is similar to getting access to Phase 2 connectors. Reviewing chapter 5, "The Art of the Connector Conversation," will help you in this section as well.

Making the Pitch
and Managing the Conversation

Most conversations tend to meander and shift organically, especially if they are informal, and there are many ways a proposal pitch and negotiation could go. As a preparation measure, it's still helpful to go into your meeting with decision makers with an agenda outline, either in mind or on paper. We recommend the agenda described below. You should recognize some of these elements from the excerpts of Angela's conversation with the documentary film maker.

Check-in and express appreciation. Engage in small talk, make a connection, and communicate your genuine appreciation that the decision maker has dedicated the time to meet with you.

Articulate your purpose and agree on a plan for the meeting. Ask if they would be open to hearing an idea you have for collaboration that you believe would be beneficial to them. As in informational interviews, you can be transparent about naming your hoped-for structure and plan for the meeting.

Articulate interests. Name their interests that you hope to meet and ask if there are any they would add or that you may have misunderstood. Draw on the paraphrasing skills discussed in chapter 2 (pages 74–76) to reflect back what the decision maker says and confirm that you're understanding their interests correctly. Then share what interests you believe working together would meet for you.

Share your yesable proposal. Frame the proposal as an option that you believe would meet their interests. You want to make it clear that if they like the proposal, you are prepared to agree to the proposal as is. Make clear also that you are interested in any adjustments they might want to make. Be sure to tweak your proposal to align with any new interests mentioned during this meeting. You may want to prepare several proposals and present whichever one seems like the best fit during the meeting or present a few and let the decision maker choose.

Adjust the proposal to best meet interests. Once you have put your proposal on the table, ask the decision maker what they think, and seek ways to make the proposal better for them and/or for you, while being careful not to make the proposal worse for either of you. This is the time to see if there's anything you've both missed in your conversation so far. Do you have other shared interests that you could find better ways to meet? Are there any interests of theirs that you overlooked before? Maybe you realize while talking that there's something they value highly that is simple for you to offer.

Define terms. Get a clear commitment and define next steps. Avoid leaving the ball in their court, since it could roll away and never be seen again. What happens next? Who is responsible for what pieces? Should you schedule a follow-up meeting, and if so, can you get that on the books before you leave the current meeting?

Appreciation. Whether the outcome of the meeting is what you wanted or not, be sure to thank the decision maker for taking the time to meet with you.

Handling Resistance and Pushback

If your yesable proposal isn't garnering the yes you'd hoped for, you can still use the conversation as an opportunity to thoughtfully explore why the decision maker is declining—which just might lead to a conversation about what *could* make an agreement work. Until you do the work of discovering their interests, you will probably not be able to smooth a rocky conversation. One of the most effective ways to diffuse pushback and get back to interests is by resisting the temptation to get defensive. Instead, reflect back what you hear from the decision maker and ask open-ended questions. "So it sounds like I misunderstood and you're not actually interested in offering kickboxing classes at your gym. Can you tell me a little bit more about what kind of exercise classes you did have in mind?"

Approach your task with the journalistic view we discussed in chapter 4 in "Committing . . . to Not Yet Committing" (page 114). This time you've been given the assignment of researching an article on the idiosyncratic business decisions of this particular decision maker. Why are they making these decisions? What is important to them? Once you've learned more about their interests, you can decide if it's worth taking another crack at making a yes-able proposal.

If a decision maker rejects your proposal, take a moment to pause. Emotional reactions subside with time, so buying yourself even just a few moments can be essential to producing a thoughtful response and continuing the conversation in a way that is productive and collaborative. You may consider excusing yourself to go to the bathroom, pausing to take notes, or simply repeating back the exact words the decision maker just said—"Oh, okay, conducting an assessment simply isn't realistic this year." This final option is a good way to maintain the conversation's flow and to buy yourself time to think. Also, by reflecting back, you convey to the connector that you have heard their rejection, and if you follow it up with an open-ended question, then you create an opportunity to gain even more information before responding.

As you delve into a conversation about a declined proposal, your response—using paraphrasing and open-ended questions—might look like one of these.

- "Based on what I proposed, you don't see hiring me as a good idea. I don't want to end up in a role that's a bad match for me either. Can you help me understand what you *would* be looking for?"
- "You have an interest in ensuring that your team is able to work efficiently, and you're concerned that bringing on someone new would be a burden. Is there anything else?"
- "So am I right in understanding that you need someone who can [work three evenings a week—restating their interest]?"

- "It seems like what matters to you is [the success of this particular product line in the next six months—restating their interest]."
- "You have [a budgetary constraint in this quarter—restating their interests]."
- "What would it take to turn your no into a yes?"

If you see an obvious way to meet any new interests the decision maker mentions in the course of this conversation, propose it. If not, you may need to regroup after the conversation and think about what you could propose that would meet their interests. If this is the case, thank the decision maker for their time, and if you think you might return to negotiate with this decision maker at a later date, leave the door open for that negotiation. Ask if they would be willing to meet with you again once you've had time to think things over, and, if it seems possible and appropriate, try to set another date before you leave.

If it is clear that there is no way for you to meet the decision maker's interests at this point, you can ask them for advice—in essence, turning the conversation into an informational interview. You can also go back to your other connectors and debrief the conversation. They can help you think through what happened and what the decision maker's interests were.

If the first conversation goes well and your decision maker accepts your proposal, you may end up negotiating compensation and other concrete terms. For more on how to handle these kinds of conversations, flip ahead to chapter 9, "Rethinking the Interview and the Offer," in Phase 3.

Acknowledging the Dynamics of Self-Advocacy

While reading this chapter, some people will think, "Well, of course I'd ask for opportunities and make proposals for what I want. I have just as much a right to be heard and to pursue my goals as anybody else." Others will think, "I'd never be able to do this. I'd be overstepping; I'd come off as arrogant or presumptuous. I can't imagine why they would say yes." In the most extreme cases, someone might think, "Asking would put my career in jeopardy. There could be major repercussions if I'm that forward." These reactions depend partly on personality, of course, but they are also informed by our experience of gender, race, age, ability, culture, social class, and other factors.

When it comes to asking for opportunities and advocating for yourself, two dynamics are at play. First, there's the internal psychological dynamic: your own degree of comfort with asking for something, which is based on your life experience, social identities, and assumptions about how the decision maker will react. Second, there's the external social dynamic: the decision maker's actual response to your requests.

In an ideal world, no one would have to fear asking, advocating, and negotiating for the opportunities they want. In the real world, where we do sometimes stand to lose out if we speak up, the first challenge is to identify which kind of resistance you're facing in a given situation. Are your fears of asking based mainly in your mindset and not on your actual interactions with decision makers? Or are you getting real pushback from decision makers? It's likely a bit of both. But understanding which one is most salient in a particular instance can help you find the right kind of support to figure out how to proceed.

When resistance to asking and negotiating for opportunities is mainly internal, you may want to consult with a friend, a therapist, or a coach. When decision makers truly do have an adverse reaction to your stepping up to negotiate for opportunities, your best course of action would be to seek out other connectors who are familiar with your field, who have faced similar challenges, who share similar social identities as you, and who have specific advice about how to deal with these setbacks.

Taking on What You Can

Two attitudes are essential for getting a solid foothold in your field. The first is an internal mindset that's especially helpful at this stage in your career: be open to almost anything This means saying yes to as many different kinds of opportunities as possible—even imperfect opportunities—whenever it feels reasonable to do so. The second is an outward demeanor that you communicate to decision makers: "No problem, I'm on it." You're looking to project an air of capability, competence, and professionalism, so that decision makers will feel comfortable offering you opportunities.

When we say, "be open to almost anything," we don't mean take absolutely everything that comes your way. You should take only the opportunities *that meet your interests in one way or another.* Let's face it, though: it's true that during Phase 2 you're still pretty low on the food chain. You don't have a lot of negotiating power yet, so you can't always afford to be picky. The opportunities you'll have access to as you start to negotiate with decision makers during Phase 2 won't meet all of your interests directly. Getting your foot in the door often requires taking on informal duties, doing unstructured internships, working evenings or weekends while you support yourself with a lackluster full-time job, doing work for less than good pay, and a myriad of other not-so-ideal arrangements.

Perhaps your goal is to be a science writer, reporting on new technologies and exciting discoveries for a broad audience in major blogs and magazines. But the only opportunities you can access right now are a technical writing job where you would help edit manuals, and an assistantship where you'd help a researcher write a journal article for a niche field with a small audience. The relevant questions to ask yourself are: "Does one of these touch on enough of my immediate interests to make it worth checking out? Will it help me develop skills and credibility I'll need later? Will I meet people who might open more appealing doors for me in the future? Is this a forum for getting noticed?"

Because you are still a newcomer to your chosen field, we

encourage you to err on the side of accepting much of what comes your way—within reason, of course. Not every opportunity will provide the money, recognition, or contacts you'd hope for. We're not advocating that you overcommit yourself, burn yourself out, or get stuck in an exploitative situation that gives very little in return. Work–life balance and respectful working conditions are important even for entry-level employees.

But if an opportunity meets any of the interests on your Interest Profile and you're able to make it work within your financial and other constraints, go for it. Rarely in Phase 2 will there be significant opportunity costs for taking on a project. One of the benefits of early modest investment opportunities is that by their nature they don't take up all of your time and energy, so they won't prevent you from taking on additional, better opportunities that might come along. If something seems beneath you, try tempering your ego and honestly evaluating whether your time and efforts will actually be wasted. Most often they won't be.

Maybe you're interested in becoming a family therapist and you've been offered an opportunity to intern or do a little part-time work as a receptionist for a divorce lawyer who sees a lot of family cases. It's not perfectly relevant, but if you don't have access to anything better, say yes anyway. It would be easy to dismiss this opportunity as "just" a boring clerical job. But it's still an avenue for learning how to work with families in crisis, what skills are needed to manage tense and emotionally fraught interactions, how the legal system affects families, and other relevant information. It may also give you the opportunity to "audition" in front of the decision maker by taking on new and challenging tasks. If you impress the lawyer, maybe she'll be a good source of referrals in the future, referring families to you for therapy once you're trained and working. The more you say yes to opportunities in Phase 2, the more you improve your chances of getting these kinds of auditions and generating additional opportunities in the future.

As a rule, in Phase 2 it's beneficial to consider a broad spectrum of opportunities and to be flexible about what you'll accept in return for your work—for instance, negotiating to receive training or mentorship if payment is not an option. We are not advocating that you take on a lot of unpaid labor. The prevalence of unpaid internships and underpaid entry-level jobs is a deeply unjust issue in our economy. But the reality is that at this early stage in your career, *access capital* is the currency that will allow you to advance in your chosen field, and sometimes the only options for building access are unpaid or underpaid. Modest investment opportunities are one way to protect yourself from the societal problem of un(der)paid labor because they don't take up all your time or prevent you from doing other, paid work—and yet they still help you build relevant access capital. Another strategy, if the pay is low or nonexistent, is to negotiate for something else that is *genuinely* valuable to you in return.

> *CARLY:* At one point on my winding journey, I connected with a psychologist who ran her own consulting business in the field of cross-cultural research and education. I was really interested in learning from Joan, and she was open to including me in some of her work, so we negotiated a simple, informal internship. For a few hours a week, I assisted with whatever she needed, such as performing background research, coordinating interviews with research participants, publicizing upcoming courses, and doing website management. Through this work, I learned about the specific subfield of cross-cultural psychology and I saw what it was like to run your own business as a solo consultant. It's true, the work I was doing was unpaid, but it was only a few, flexible hours a week, so I could easily fit it in around my paid jobs. Plus, we set up a valuable barter agreement: after working with her for six months, I could attend one of her intensive, weekend-long training seminars for free—a useful and relevant learning opportunity that would otherwise have cost me thousands of dollars.

In addition to maintaining a sustainable work-life balance for your own well-being, there are also practical limits to being open to almost anything. You need to make sure you can do all of the work well, particularly in situations where others depend on you and where your performance may lead to a reference or could affect your reputation. Furthermore, if you take an opportunity in order to build or practice skills, you owe it to yourself to make the most of it. If you're overbooked and overworked, you run the risk of burning out, double booking, having to cancel, or, worse, outright forgetting to show up for a commitment. This is why now, as you take on more and more responsibilities, it's important to recognize your limits.

The essential purpose of projecting an "I'm on it" attitude is to get decision makers to think of you as a standout, reliable person so that they'll feel comfortable delegating work to you and recommending you to others. If decision makers get to know you as someone who constantly says yes to the opportunities they offer, and who has a "no-problem" attitude about figuring out how to get things done, *and* as someone who consistently follows through in delivering quality work, they're more likely to keep involving you. During his Phase 2, Tad began as one of many volunteer mediators working for a local mediation firm. In the course of this work, he noticed that the firm had a particular problem, and by helping them address it, he started to stand out from the pack and his superiors took note.

> *TAD:* After I had decided to become a professional mediator and had taken my basic mediation training, I was volunteering for a local dispute resolution firm by mediating in the Massachusetts district courts. At the time, I was also running my own marketing company, so I mediated during the day a few times a week and did marketing work during the other days and at night. I mediated approximately eighty-five cases in a year, which gave me plenty of practice, but it was all on a volunteer basis. I was still trying to figure out how to break into a paid job as a mediator, so I continued doing informational interviews with connectors in the field. My connectors told me that certain courts were often understaffed and short of mediators because they were in remote suburbs and far from public transportation.

The firm had an interest in maintaining good relationships with *all* the courthouses, but that was tough when they had trouble providing volunteer mediators in the faraway locations. So I started to call the firm's program manager each week and to ask, "Where do you need a mediator on Wednesday?" I was hoping that by my being willing to trek out to the distant courthouses, the firm would start to see me as their problem-solving person.

Tad's willingness to put in extra work to serve the out-of-the-way locations, backed up by his strong mediation skill and growing track record of good results, made him a go-to mediator for the firm. Eventually, the program manager started assigning Tad even more mediation opportunities, as well as higher-profile, paid cases.

A Note about Staying Organized

Early on in your phase 2 work, you will likely be able to handle all of your appointments, preparation for meetings with connectors, and follow-ups by memory. As you become more successful in finding and engaging connectors, and as your access capital grows, you will need to get organized. In almost any industry you might be trying to break into, being able to demonstrate strong organizational skills—such as showing up early to your appointments, remembering all of your commitments, and following through on each one—will go a long way toward building a reputation for yourself as someone who is reliable and easy to work with. The tough moment comes when you realize you need a better organizational system but you no longer have time to develop one because you're so busy with work and connectors.

Our advice is to take some time to get yourself organized *before* you really need to. You will not regret carving out a couple of days to figure out an organization system that works for you before your life becomes chaotic as you become more successful in your phase 2 endeavors. There are many great systems out there. You have to find something that works for you personally. We recommend doing a mini set of connector conversations to supplement whatever research you do on getting organized. We have found that these three things make the biggest difference in staying organized:

- Having a way to capture in one place all ideas, commitments, and to-do's as they come in. This could be a little notebook, a note on your phone, or scrap paper on your desk.
- Holding time every day to transfer your ideas, commitments, and to-do's from the place where you capture them into your organizational system so they don't get lost.
- Reviewing your to-do lists, calendars, and big projects every week to make sure nothing is falling through the cracks.

Managing Opportunities That Are Over Your Head

As a standout person, you want to continue to be open to almost anything and say "Yes!" But what if you are offered opportunities that are beyond your ability? Accepting challenging work beyond your comfort zone forces you to learn and grow. Even more, meeting the challenges successfully is an effective way to build confidence and make upward progress in your career. It involves risk, however. Where is the line between exciting and dangerous, rewarding and draining, quality outcomes and underperforming, responsible and irresponsible?

When you are considering an opportunity that's over your head, you have three options: turn down the opportunity, fake it as best you can on your own and potentially blow it, or reach out to connectors to ask for help. Doing it alone is often a good way to fail. We recommend asking for help. Ask your connectors how this task is usually approached in the field. What are the expectations? How can you quickly build your skills in the limited time you have? How would leaders in the field handle this opportunity? With your connectors behind you, and with a good understanding of your own interests, the operant question doesn't have to be, "Am I up for this?" It should be, "What support and resources would it take for me to nail this?" Answer that question first and then decide whether it's worth it to you (that is, whether it meets your interests) to seek out and secure the support and resources you need to excel in the opportunity. Doing your homework, asking connectors for advice and help, and soliciting continual feedback allows you to keep a constant pulse on your performance and to make sure you're delivering high-quality work. Knowing that you have good mentors and advisers to rely on helps mitigate the emotional strain of taking on a high level of risk. During Phase 2, Justin got so used to projecting a confident, can-do attitude, that he was often offered projects that stretched his novice abilities. He quickly learned that asking for collaborative input from connectors was the best way to manage these "What have I gotten myself into?" situations.

> *JUSTIN:* Shortly after being trained as a mediator, a
> decision maker asked if I would be willing to run a
> mediation training workshop for a farming cooperative
> in rural Mexico. I enthusiastically agreed to take on the
> project, never having done anything like this before. I
> approached several of my connectors and asked for their
> advice on designing and running workshops, and asked for
> their blessing to translate some of their case examples into
> Spanish to use in the training.
>
> With their advice, I put together an agenda, which
> I took to another connector. He pointed out that getting
> people to participate was going to be one of my biggest
> challenges, given that many of my attendees, while brilliant
> farmers, had only middle school educations and were not
> used to classroom learning. So we redesigned the workshop
> around small-group activities. This was an invaluable
> change. The mediation workshop, which I never could
> have done alone so early in my career, was a success thanks

to my willingness to ask for and follow the advice of my connectors.

Negotiating with decision makers in Phase 2 can lead to these kinds of exciting, challenging, growth-inducing opportunities that allow you to get your foot in the door of your chosen field. Drawing on the advice, knowledge, and collaboration of your connectors can help you make the most of these Phase 2 opportunities.

When you identify the field you want to dive into at the end of Phase 1, it can be tempting to skip over Phase 2 and immediately put all your energy into finding your dream job. But most of us don't have the access capital we need to get that dream job without first undertaking an intentional, proactive effort to build access by talking with connectors and seeking out modest investment opportunities to get a foothold in the field.

If you truly allow yourself to spend time in Phase 2 and engage in the activities that we've outlined in this chapter, you'll have built your access capital to the point that you're now a strong candidate for the jobs you really want. You'll have the confidence of knowing that you understand the landscape of the field you want to enter, and you will have the skills, qualifications, and relationships required to have a strong reputation. You will also know where you best fit because you've tested out different kinds of roles in your field.

Now it's time to go after that job that will love you back!

Getting Work You Love

Conversations with DECISION MAKERS

7

Time to Focus

Your most critical negotiations in Phase 3, Getting Work You Love, are with the decision makers who can offer you opportunities to do the work you love. You'll get there soon! For now, you're fresh out of Phase 2—which, for many people, can be a chaotic, arduous, uncertain period—and the move into Phase 3 calls for some negotiation with yourself. You're no longer merely struggling to get your foot in the door of your chosen field; you've crossed the threshold and you're thinking about what's next for you on the other side. How do you go from gaining access to doing the work you want to do most? How do you move from being the intern, green hire, or newbie on the scene to respected team member, seasoned expert, or headline act?

Negotiating with yourself in Phase 3 is a two-pronged effort. First, you'll reevaluate your Interest Profile based on the experience, knowledge, and access you gained during Phase 2. Second, once you're clear on your *current* interests and access capital, you will set your sights on some ambitious, achievable target opportunities for doing the work you really want to do. You'll shift your mindset from saying yes to just about everything to an attitude that is more selective as you begin to pursue ideal job opportunities that are now within your reach.

To give you a better sense of what this looks like, let's take a look at Keychette's transition from Phase 2 to Phase 3. Keychette was interested in sustainable farming and also had some writing and basic graphic design skills. As she was nearing the end of Phase 2, she managed to get into a learning exchange with a farming co-op, where she took classes in exchange for helping create the farm's website and marketing materials. She did such a good job that other farms, markets, and sustainable food stores started to hear about her work. She eventually found herself with a constant flow of marketing and social media gigs, including a few paid opportunities. Because she was in a Phase 2 mindset, Keychette said yes to almost all the marketing and communications opportunities that came her way. Over time, these opportunities allowed her to meet her Phase 2 interests. She gained a thorough sense of the landscape of sustainable farming. She earned a basic living. She continued to take free classes and volunteered at the farming co-op, where she accumulated knowledge and skills in soil science, animal husbandry, operating farm machinery, and cultivating a variety of crops. And, she developed relationships with connectors and decision makers.

As Keychette found herself writing the co-op's monthly newsletters and web content, managing social media for three farms, designing jam jar labels for a berry producer, doing advertising for the local farmers market, meeting with connectors, volunteering in the greenhouses, taking a class on tractor maintenance at the co-op, and managing a myriad of other tasks, Keychette had more work than she could handle. She should have probably dropped some of these opportunities, but it was not immediately clear which ones she should hold on to. Plus, people were starting to count on her, and she was worried about letting them down. Overall, this setup was okay, but she was exhausted from the number of balls she was trying to keep in the air—and she was not actually very passionate about much of the work she was doing. She still didn't feel like she was "there."

Feeling stuck, Keychette reevaluated her Interest Profile, realizing that the two main interests that attracted her to sustainable farming were doing hands-on, outdoor work and directly making change in the dysfunctional food production system. If she didn't make a deliberate move toward doing actual agricultural work, she could find herself pigeonholed into a career on the sidelines of sustainable agriculture, never moving beyond her Phase 2 access work—the marketing and communications contracts that she originally sought as a means to get her foot in the door.

Keychette wrapped up most of her marketing and communications gigs and accepted no new offers, using the extra time to take stock of her access capital, research target job opportunities, and begin a comprehensive job search. She continued to do some communications work for the co-op so that she could still take classes there because she prioritized this valuable opportunity for building her skills. By this point, Keychette had banked some solid access capital that gave her the leverage she needed to move into Phase 3. Not only did she have lots of connections in the field, but her marketing success had attached a positive reputation to her name, and decision makers viewed her as sharp and hardworking. She had basic hands-on skills, and by working closely with farm managers in the course of her marketing jobs, she'd gained a good understanding of what owners and managers value in their crews. Furthermore, on her roster of current communications tasks, Keychette managed a website where job openings were posted. Hence, she had a good sense of who was hiring and what types of openings were available—and often heard about them before anyone else did.

She was eventually hired as a crew member at an organic vegetable farm. On a day-to-day basis, she's now doing the work she loves. She's outside planting, harvesting, and learning. She's responsible for selling veggies at farmers markets and feels good about being able to offer people healthy, sustainably grown food. This is Phase 3, but she's still in the earliest stage. The pay isn't great, and she isn't yet in a place where she can enact some of the larger changes she wants to see, like supporting the women's leadership in agriculture and providing affordable farm-fresh produce to communities in food deserts. But she will work toward meeting these interests and goals as she progresses through Phase 3. When she has more experience under her belt, Keychette plans to set her sights on farm manager positions—the ideal role she'll pursue when she's nearing the end of Phase 3. Later, she will pursue her Phase 4 project: realizing her dream of becoming a farmer-activist on a regional scale.

The burst of effort and activity that Keychette put into her Phase 2 allowed her to accumulate the access capital she needed to enter Phase 3. Yet, it wasn't immediately clear to her how she should make the shift from Phase 2 to Phase 3. She needed to take some time to step back and negotiate with herself at the beginning of Phase 3 in order to make an intentional plan of action. Reevaluating her Interest Profile allowed her to whittle down her various modest investment opportunities and begin to pursue one or two fulfilling gigs where she can do the work she loves.

Taking Stock and Identifying New Targets

Reaching Phase 3 means you're ready to make a serious commitment to the work you love. The first step is getting clear on precisely what that looks like. Many job hunters end up on paths that don't satisfy their interests because they failed to engage in this kind of mid-journey reflection. Does your Interest Profile still hold up, or has experience shifted things? Think again about the ends you're aiming for. What still drives you? Perfecting your craft, working within a dynamic team, being free from busywork, covering your family's expenses, maintaining a good work-life balance? Reconfirming your interests will help you make difficult choices between competing job commitments and emerging opportunities.

Revising Your Interest Profile

Take the time to sit down and revise your Interest Profile based on the experiences you had in Phase 2. What kinds of work did you find most fulfilling? Why was it fulfilling? Did any of your conversations with connectors or decision makers change how you view your career ambitions or the roads to realizing those ambitions? Be ruthlessly honest. It's entirely possible that some of the interests you identified earlier will seem naive or incomplete to you now; you were in the right ballpark, but you didn't know which team to cheer for. Or maybe your interests still stand, but they're now in a different order. It's also quite possible that other aspects of your life have changed since the last time you revised your Interest Profile. Maybe you got married and kids are now on the horizon. The work you want to do hasn't changed, but entering Phase 3 with new needs and motivations, earning a salary that can support a family, has jumped to the top spot on your Interest Profile.

Many people find it helpful not only to list their interests, but to rank them from highest to lowest priority—or at least identify their top five or ten—to better reflect how each interest relates to the others. The desired outcome of revising your Interest Profile now is an honest, deliberate inventory of your current interests, which you can use to help you decide which target job opportunities to go after in Phase 3.

Tallying Your Access Capital

As you revise your Interest Profile, take stock of the access capital you've acquired thus far. What skills, connections, and social capital have you built up to this point? What have you learned about your field, such as how decisions are made, what is valued, who the most influential people are, and which decision makers hold the keys to your most coveted jobs? Do you have any unique insights into the workings and landscape of the field? What abilities and competencies have you developed that are of special interest to decision makers? Make a list of everything that has helped you—and may continue to help you—make progress in your field.

All of this access capital will now be part of your story. To strategically determine your next steps, you'll need to pull it all together explicitly. The key question to consider is: How can I use my access capital to get the kinds of job offers, projects, workflow, and standing that I want?

Anticipating Your Options
and Setting Targets

In the early stages of Phase 3, you'll want to aim for several target jobs or opportunities that entail the kinds of work you're really excited about. At least two. Try to narrow down your options to specific roles that you would like to have in specific companies or organizations. Or, use your knowledge of the field's landscape to imagine specific, realistic freelance or independent roles. For now, make a list of as many of these options as you can without any ranking or judging them. Aim high!

When you've made that list, weigh the options according to how well they meet your interests. It might be difficult for you to foresee with confidence how well each one might meet your interests. After all, these are jobs and companies you may still know little about. Do your best. As you gain more information, you'll have time later in Phase 3 to continue evaluating your target options. Next, consider each role on your list in terms of constraints: Is geography a factor? Are there skills or experiences you may still need in order to be a viable candidate? Considering these constraints will help you judge the attainability of each option for the short, medium, and long term.

Balancing your enthusiasm for each option with its attainability is an important part of short-listing your options. Target a set of jobs that includes both the ones you are most excited about and ones you are likely to get. It can be hard to know how likely you are to attain the options you are pursuing. Fortunately, your connectors can help you get clarity about your chances. You want to keep a few options open until you have a committed job offer that satisfies your highest-priority interests. Focus is good, but it's risky to depend on a single option to meet all of your interests. The future is uncertain, and even the most promising opportunities can fall through, so you'll be more likely to fulfill your interests if you always view each potential job or opportunity as one of several possibilities, rather than *the* ideal job. Also, when you're negotiating with a specific decision maker for a particular role you've targeted, having alternatives—other viable offers—gives you power. One of the main sources of bargaining power in any negotiation is the strength of your alternatives.

As you enter Phase 3, it's important to pay more attention to your negotiating power. For instance, if you have an internship at Disney and you want to negotiate for a full-time job there, your bargaining power will be stronger if you get offered another internship at another company where you also really want to work—or, better yet, an offer of another full-time job. Then, when you set out to negotiate with Disney, you'll have the power to say, "I'd love to work here—and I hope you'll understand that it only makes sense for me to stay here if we can devise a better package than what I've been offered by [the other company]." If you don't have any other offers, then you will not have as much negotiating power to persuade decision makers to meet your interests.

When we discuss negotiating with Phase 3 decision makers in chapter 9, "Rethinking the Interview and the Offer," we will talk in greater detail about different ways to use your negotiating power to influence decision makers. For now, we raise this point because it can be tempting to put all of your focus on a single dream job. There might be two—or more!

Revisiting Your Story

Once you've retooled your Interest Profile, taken stock of your access capital, and begun to target specific jobs, what do you do with this information? Your immediate next step is to speak with connectors about other targets they recommend and what advice they have for landing those jobs and the ones you have identified. The best way to pull together your revised interests, access capital, and target goals is to return to the story-building exercise we introduced in chapter 2,

"Bringing Out Your Story," and revisited in chapter 5, "The Art of the Connector Conversation." Remember the five core elements of your story: biographical information, passion, interests, constraints, and a call for support—the all-important ask.

In Phase 3, your story's structure remains the same, but the content needs to be updated to reflect your current circumstances. Consider how each element of your story will need reframing or refreshing to communicate where you are now and where you want to go in Phase 3. As in every phase, the specifics of your story and your ultimate ask will change. In Phase 3, when negotiating with connectors, your ask will center on how to get—and excel in—your target opportunities, and when negotiating with decision makers, you will be negotiating for a job, for the specific terms that will best fit your interests.

Shifting Your Mindset from "Do It All" to "Do It If"

The line between Phase 2 and 3 is not always crystal clear. There might be a watershed moment where you're launched from part-time secretary into your Phase 3 dream job of full-time business manager. But for many people, the transition from Phase 2 to Phase 3 entails a fuzzier, slower shift. Justin was doing freelance work in the conflict resolution field during Phases 2 *and* 3, but the substance of his freelance work changed as he moved into Phase 3.

> *JUSTIN:* During my Phase 2, my freelance gigs consisted of doing background research for mediation consultants, taking notes during facilitations, and marketing a negotiation firm's services—low-paying, ad hoc opportunities that didn't allow me to do much actual conflict resolution work. As my access capital grew and my bargaining power improved, I slowly began to fill my schedule with more of the work I loved—and thereby gradually shifted into Phase 3. I got hired to mediate complex, interesting cases and to lead negotiation trainings.

I designed curricula and created exercises. I also got the chance to work with experts in the field, spending my workdays with people who challenged my thinking and pushed me to grow.

In Keychette's case, the move into Phase 3 didn't simply happen. She could have continued to accept every new access opportunity that came her way, focusing on meeting her marketing deadlines while squeezing in classes and volunteer hours on the farm. But if she had gotten stuck in this pattern, she never would have had the bandwidth to reevaluate her interests, identify new job targets, or engage in a time-consuming hunt for paid, hands-on farm crew jobs. Once she had accrued enough access capital and clarity about her interests, Keychette had to deliberately stop the Phase 2 quest for access and shift her mindset—turning down the marketing work that was no longer meeting her interests in order to propel herself into Phase 3.

In Phase 3 your mindset shifts to one of discernment and thoughtful cost-benefit analysis. You're prioritizing opportunities that meet the core work-related needs and desires that make up your Interest Profile or, at the very least, opportunities that constitute a clear, deliberate step toward your desired targets.

At first glance, making this mindset shift may seem simple. If you've spent a long time—possibly years—in Phase 2, however, it can be hard to turn off the impulse to say yes to every interest-ing opportunity. You might be worried about letting people down. You might have been highly recommended for a prestigious post and feel too flattered to say no, even though it's not on your ideal career path. You might be resistant to giving up a contract that pays particularly well, despite the fact that it doesn't move you toward your target jobs. The "do it all" attitude you fostered in Phase 2 can be especially difficult to leave behind because it's easy to fear that your progress will come to a complete halt. Even with a clear sense of your interests and priorities, the transition into Phase 3 will likely test your ability to say no and to discern the best option.

Perhaps a particularly attractive job meets a lot of your interests, but it requires you to relinquish your current appointment, which is already a pretty good fit. Opportunity costs can be hard to calculate, and we can't give you a hard-and-fast rule for how to handle these moments. Fortunately, your Interest Profile will be a trusty guide. It provides you with a reliable tool for evaluating the fit of any given opportunity as you work your way toward excellent job offers.

8

The "Asks" That Will Get You In

In the transition from Phase 2 to Phase 3—from gaining access to doing the work you love—your needs and aims in meeting with connectors shift. Although it's the decision makers you meet with next in Phase 3 who will grant or deny you entry to your target jobs, it's your connectors who help you lock down those targets and excel in your work.

You might reasonably wonder why we are insisting that you still need the assistance of connectors even if you have your targets and know how to go after them. Here's why. For starters, connectors can help you leverage your access capital to get specific jobs or opportunities. You'll likely still need information from connectors about what your target decision makers care about. Connectors in Phase 3 are also a fount of advice, support, and assistance as you begin taking on ambitious opportunities that bring you deeper into the work you love—and possibly out of your depth, beyond your current skills and abilities.

In all likelihood, many of the connectors whose wisdom you benefited from in Phases 1 and 2 can still help you in Phase 3. Your established connectors know and trust you and are more likely to go out on a limb to support you. Of course, that's not to say that you shouldn't reach out to new connectors; your Phase 3 work will put you in close proximity to new people who could also become your most relevant connectors. Given that what you need from connectors varies throughout Phase 3, it is reasonable to expect that you will need to draw on a diverse group of them. You might meet with one person to help you decide exactly which target job opportunities to pursue. Another connector might help you figure out how to complete a project that's a bit over your head. Yet another can help you prepare for an interview at one of your target companies.

Because you're looking for different things from each connector, your asks will depend on context. This section focuses on (1) strategizing around your targets and (2) seeking assistance with a project—the two primary reasons for approaching connectors in Phase 3.

Focus Your Ask
to Get That Ideal Job

Early in Phase 3, seek strategic advice from connectors anytime you are either unsure of which of a number of target opportunities to focus on or struggling to pinpoint specific job targets. Both reflect times when you are struggling to add specifics to your path and you need help clarifying and zeroing in on your targets. Your ask here is to have a conversation where you can bounce ideas off a veteran in the field. Seek connectors who will readily be able to assess which specific jobs, projects, clients, or roles will best meet your interests, and will help you brainstorm alternative targets if your initial ideas are off the mark.

Of course, if they don't already know you, you'll first have to share your updated story in order to set up your ask. Even if they do already know you, it's still helpful to let them know how your interests and access capital have evolved. This is where you can draw on your recently updated story.

In such cases, your ask might look something like this:
- [After telling your story] From what I know so far, the workplaces I'm considering are X, Y, and Z. Based on my interests, Y seems like it might be the best firm for

me, although I'm still not exactly sure what specific roles
I should be looking for. Based on your knowledge of the
field, does that sound right?

- Are there any other opportunities you would recommend
  I look into that did not make my list? [Give them a
  chance to brainstorm with you.]
- Which of these do you think will best meet my interests,
  and which will not?
- If you were me, where would you start?

If you are really struggling to limit the set of targets to pursue,
you may need to meet with several connectors specifically for the
purpose of choosing targets. On the other hand, if you're confident
in your direction and target options, you can skip on to the next set
of questions, which address how to hit your targets.

Even with a clear direction and confidence that your targets
are solid, you will need connectors' wisdom to figure out the best
way to pursue them. The first thing to discern is: Who is the decision maker for your target job, role, or opportunity? Next you will
want to check in with your connectors about the specific cultures
and hiring practices associated with your target opportunities, as
well as the decision makers' interests and quirks. Your connectors
can give you insight into what to expect from a given hiring process or from a negotiation with a certain decision maker. Likewise,
your connectors' knowledge can also assist you in crafting yesable
proposals. At the outset of Phase 3, your negotiations might focus
on getting hired, while later on you might negotiate with decision
makers around taking on new clients, getting a raise, or any number
of aspects within your new job.

With this as your purpose, your ask could take a few different
forms. Something like:

- [After your story] I'm looking at X and Z as the two
  opportunities that will best meet my interests and
  allow me to do work I'm genuinely passionate about.
  Given what I told you about my background and the

connections I've been fortunate enough to make [offer specifics about your access capital], if you were me, what would you do to go after these opportunities?

- Who makes the decisions about these opportunities?
- What do they care about?
- Can you think of anything I could do or say that might make them more receptive?
- Is there anyone else you can recommend I contact who could share some insight into how one gets these kinds of opportunities?

In some cases, a single connector might lay out a clear and helpful path for how to meet with your target decision maker and how to negotiate your ideal job with that person. At other times, you might not get a clear sense of how to go after your targets until you've pieced together information from numerous connectors.

Be mindful that some connectors may have an outdated or skewed sense of how hiring and advancement in the field currently works. Information from many connectors is always preferable— that's why it's important that your ask include a request for recommendations for other people you can approach with your questions.

Excellence Is About Finding Support

As you progress into Phase 3, you're likely to have the opportunity to work on projects or be hired for jobs that are beyond the scope of your current skills and experience. These opportunities will come from your negotiations with decision makers for your target opportunities. They may also come naturally from the momentum you built up when you were negotiating with decision makers in Phase 2 to gain access. As always, you want to exceed client or supervisor expectations. If you start to push for a project or level of responsibility that you know may be over your head, you will need to understand what necessary experience and skills you are lacking, and what to do about it. Again, if an opportunity exceeds your competence or skill set, that shouldn't automatically dissuade you from taking it on. Your meetings with connectors can focus on figuring out how you can excel in these cases where you're taking a calculated risk.

You may not know what you are missing, or exactly what questions to ask, and need the connector to help guide you through a conversation about what skills, mindsets, or subtleties lead to excellence in this field. If you're looking to become a floor electrician for a ballet company, you probably know that you need electrician's training and credentials, maybe union membership, and a general knowledge of theater. You may not know, however, that you need to be intimately familiar with the music and dance routines in a particular performance so you can predict the comings and goings of performers and place yourself accordingly as you prepare to make set adjustments. Only certain connectors with similar experience can help you realize this kind of gap in your understanding and help you do an outstanding job right off the bat.

Connector assistance can make the difference between doing acceptable work and exemplary work. To get the best advice possible, you want to meet with connectors who themselves do exemplary work and are leaders in the field. If none of your current connectors do the work you have been tasked with, find out if they can connect you with someone who does, and does it well. Having their support and guidance will be well worth the effort.

When speaking to these connectors, your call for support— your ask—will be mainly focused on the task at hand. As always, you will need to share enough of your story so that the connector understands who you are and why this opportunity—and doing it well—matters to you. And then, make your request.

- [After your story] All this has culminated in my getting the chance to do X. I'm excited and nervous because I know how important it is to do a good job. Given what I've shared about my background and interests, what would you do if you were in my shoes and you wanted to do a great job at this?
- How would you design and/or execute this job to best meet the supervisor's/client's expectations?

- What resources or support might you seek to ensure the work is excellent?
- What are the most common mistakes you see when people do this kind of work for the first time?
- Would you be open to me checking back in with you as the project progresses if I have any strategic questions about how to proceed?

The transition into Phase 3 will likely require you to take some risks and step outside your comfort zone. Taking on challenging opportunities—that sometimes exceed your current skills—is not about hubris or overestimating your abilities. It's about a commitment to finding the assistance you need to build the necessary skills. Next, we'll look at the specific ways you might ask your connectors for support during Phase 3.

Getting Their Direct Collaboration

It can also happen that you just don't have the skills and experience you need to excel on a project and there simply isn't enough time for you to acquire this know-how. What then? You could turn down the work. You could take it on alone and fail miserably. Or you could consult with a colleague, mentor, or other connector and ask for assistance in completing the project. Working with an expert almost guarantees that you will exceed expectations. Not only that, but this kind of on-the-job or project-specific training from a seasoned professional will expand your skills and abilities for the future.

Your ask—your call for support—on specific projects could take one of four forms.

First, you could ask for advice in thinking through your process for executing a project. For example, a new hire at a company that does energy audits for homes could be tasked with creating a survey to analyze the effectiveness of one of the company's programs. He manages a team of three people and has never set up a research project like this before. He could reach out to a connector who is an academic and oversees research teams and ask if she would be willing to discuss his survey plan and to share suggestions about how he might manage his team.

Second, your ask could be for direct feedback on your work product. A new journalist could be asked to write a story about a politically controversial decision made by the State Supreme Court regarding a new immigration law. She knows that the framing of this article is critically important and wants to get it right. She could approach a close friend of hers who has worked as a political journalist for many years, to ask if he would be willing to read her article and give feedback on the framing before she sends it to her managing editor. The political journalist has an interest in promoting more thoughtful, unbiased articles about immigration in the media, so he could be glad to give feedback.

Third, you may ask a connector to collaborate with you on a project. A freelance designer who has been hired to create a prototype for the body of a new luxury sports car might reach out to one of the professors he had in design school who specialized in aerodynamic design and ask if she would be willing to work with him on making a 3-D digital image. He asks this particular professor because he knows that she rarely does commercial work anymore and likes to get back in touch with it from time to time. Plus, the designer could offer to credit the professor when he finally presents the design.

And fourth, there may be cases where you need to ask a connector to take over a project completely or in part. A graduate student teaching their first class on urban planning could be asked to include one lecture on leadership. Between all of the work of setting up and managing a new class and all of their thesis deadlines, they do not have the time to compose a compelling lecture on leadership. They ask several colleagues if they know anyone willing to guest lecture for this session. After a few dead ends, one colleague introduces them to a connector who is a local senior city planner. Guest lecturing could meet the city planner's interests because she's trying to steer her career toward academia and build a reputation as a teacher and thought leader.

So how do you make it attractive for a more-experienced colleague to work with you? Remember yesable proposals from chapter 6 in Phase 2? Here is another golden opportunity to make connectors a proposal that meets *their* interests so that it's easier to sell them on meeting *your* interests. Often, if you approach them respectfully, honor their expertise, speak to their career passions, and appeal to your past relationship, they will agree to support you on your projects.

Becoming a Connector

Because you have gained access to a field and established yourself as a reliable colleague in it, others trying to enter the field will notice you or be sent your way by colleagues—maybe even by *your* connectors. It's important for you to recognize that you've put in a lot of work—in terms of both the job-hunt process and the actual work to have reached this point. You've put a lot of effort into identifying your interests, gathering a network of connectors, building access capital, and doing a variety of stepping-stone tasks and jobs to get where you are. And because of that work, you have a lot to offer other job hunters. Take the opportunity to pay back into your field some of that goodwill that you benefited from when you were seeking the support of connectors. You can transform the job hunt for those who view *you* as a connector by helping them (1) see where they are in the four phases, (2) recognize and prioritize their interests, and (3) plan their advancement. They will in turn, we hope, help those who ask them.

As a connector, you will often be one of the newcomers' first sources of information about the field. Your advice will inform how newcomers perceive and understand the field, and thus you may ultimately help to shape the field itself. One tiny piece of what-I-wish-I-knew-when-I-was-starting-out advice might drastically improve a newcomer's chances of success. If you can welcome someone into an otherwise unwelcoming field, you will be making a small change that could eventually improve the culture of your field. A major theme in this book is the overarching goal of creating communities and support networks. If you're going to make great strides in your own career, to the point that you can help others by becoming a connector, you need to involve others in your story and be involved in the success of others. Helping to build a connected, collaborative work environment for someone else contributes to your own sense of fulfillment in your work life.

By conscientiously acting as a connector for someone, you are likely also generating opportunities and advantages for yourself, though this may not be immediately obvious. When you connect people to other people, or people to information or ideas, you're not getting something directly out of it. Still, the people you help as a connector may down the line be able to offer you valuable connections or collaboration opportunities. In other words, you're not only paying back goodwill; you're also paying forward into potential collaboration.

In your role as a connector, you also have the chance to make connections for some of your more experienced colleagues—people who have been connectors and decision makers in your career process. You are not likely to be connecting your superiors to jobs, big opportunities, or industry leaders just yet. But if you know what your superiors are up to, you can connect them to information, relevant events, potential interns or hires, or other resources. When you come across a resource that could meet one of your superior's interests, let them know. Of course, use careful judgment about whether it's appropriate in a given situation. This will help keep you top of mind and also make it more likely that they will eventually return the favor by connecting you to something of value to you. The more you act as connector, the more you'll become known as a well-connected, knowledgeable person who contributes to your field.

9

Rethinking the Interview and the Offer

Phase 3 is about getting and doing a job that you genuinely love. In the process of landing that job, you'll be working to build quality offers from multiple target job opportunities. Building strong alternatives—offers from other organizations—will increase your negotiating power and help you avoid accepting a subpar offer. You're not just looking to land a job that's a good fit on paper; you're going to negotiate the best version of that job that you can. Much of your success will depend on how you generate and manage job interviews, and so the bulk of this chapter is dedicated to the what and how of job offer conversations.

"How to do the job interview" is probably the most thoroughly covered topic in job search literature, so what could we possibly add to this mountain of resources? We view the job interview not as a one-way screening process in which you ask for a job and a decision maker says yes or no, but rather as a two-way negotiation about whether this job can be a good arrangement *for both of you*. To do this, we reconceptualize the interview process as a series of conversations about fit and interests.

There are three basic steps to negotiating for work: (1) getting in the room with a decision maker, (2) evaluating fit, for you and the decision maker, and (3) negotiating an offer. Whether the steps happen in the same conversation or take place over several meetings, it's important to think of this negotiation process as having three discrete steps and to give each one the thought and preparation it deserves.

Before taking you through each step and recommending ways to approach and execute them, we'd first like to say a little more about building alternative job offers and why this is so integral to your securing a single, optimal job offer.

Alternatives Give You Power

In a negotiation, your alternatives are the other possible ways you can meet your interests outside the specific negotiation you're currently having. If you are negotiating for a job as the manager of research and development at Shine Finger Paints, Inc., and you have another offer from Zissor's Scissors Co., then the offer from Zissor's Scissors Co. is your alternative while you are in a meeting with Shine Finger Paints. When you go to talk with Zissor's Scissors Co., the Shine Finger Paints offer is your alternative. The better your alternatives compare to the offer you are negotiating in the moment, the more empowered you'll be in asking for what you want and the more comfortable you'll be walking away if you don't get it.

To see how alternatives give you power, imagine you're applying for a job at a local tech start-up. You are enthusiastic about this job because you have an interest in being involved in something daring on the cutting edge. You also want to work there because you know two of the team members well and have collaborated with them on past projects. Working at this company would meet your interest of being part of a dynamic and collegial work environment. Consider two potential scenarios.

Scenario 1. You have one offer from the start-up for $46,000/year with no benefits and no equity. The CEO explained to you that they are in a period between funding rounds and can't afford to pay you more. At this point, you have been job hunting for four months and don't have any other options lined up.

Scenario 2. You have multiple offers, including the one just described above. Your first alternative is a well-established company that does less innovative work but has a staff that you respect. This company is willing to pay you $85,000/year with benefits. Your second alternative is a start-up in an early stage of development. You don't know many people there yet, but they're willing to give you 1 percent equity after the first round of funding in six months and would be willing to pay you $40,000 per year until then, at which point you'd renegotiate your salary.

Which situation would you rather be in? In Scenario 2 you have choices and significantly more control. You have alternatives that clarify and reinforce your ability to turn down offers or to improve the one you most favor. Of the three offers as they stand now, maybe you end up favoring the company that offers you more equity if part of what you desire is ownership in the company where you work. With these strong alternatives, you could go back to the first company and share with them that you have an offer from another start-up that includes equity. You could make the case that, in order for you to consider taking the job, they would need to add equity into the equation.

Having alternatives significantly empowers you in negotiations: You have more power over how your interests get met *and* you can advocate for yourself with more confidence and less stress.

In fact, power in negotiation is partly defined by having at least one attractive alternative to the offer you are negotiating, which could also be staying in your current role. If the other party wants to make a deal and they know you have other offers, they're more likely to work with you on your terms. Your goal is to *create* the best offer you can by making them aware of what you need, pointing out what you could get elsewhere—not as a threat, but as information—and then inviting them to respond. For employment, the best offer is defined by the terms that best meet your interests, whether they are met through mentorship, compensation, job title, physical location, education benefits, international travel, vacation allowance, or anything else you value.

Another source of power and leverage in negotiation is how well you can meet the decision maker's interests compared to *their* next best alternative. When you're in a job interview, a decision maker's alternatives are generally other applicants for the job, or not hiring anyone. As always, understanding what the decision maker needs, and tailoring your expectations and proposals to meet their needs, can set you apart from other applicants and make it much more likely they will work with you to improve the overall terms and fit of a job offer.

What really matters is the quality of the offers you are choosing between, not the number of alternative offers you rack up. *One strong alternative is worth more than a handful of mediocre ones.* Having many alternatives that you're not serious about does not help you. What you want in a negotiation is to have at least one attractive alternative that you would be happy to take.

The best way to cultivate simultaneous opportunities is to make strong use of your connections and your knowledge of the landscape. Keep up with your connectors, keep a finger on the pulse of current events within your field, and keep following leads. You should be asking yourself, "What are my possibilities?" until you have two real offers. While the ideal scenario is to have several attractive offers on the table at the same time, job offers don't grow on trees. You may not always have the luxury of delaying your decision about one offer while you hunt for another. You may instead have only leads, not fully developed alternatives.

Let's say you have an interview next week at Shine Finger Paints, Inc., and currently have no other concrete offers. Thanks to your interactions with connectors, however, you're fairly certain that Slate Chalkboard Builders will probably have some job openings soon, and you heard through the grapevine that a podcast you were featured on impressed the Slate Chalkboard's CEO. Going into the Shine Finger Paints interview with this knowledge—vague as it may be—is more helpful than having no alternative whatsoever. You may not have a strong alternative to bargain with, but you can at least go into the interview with a good lead on one, which will inform your mindset in the Shine Finger Paints meeting. It will put you in a better mindset to evaluate any offer Shine Finger Paints might make you—and you'll be less inclined to accept a subpar offer out of desperation, if Shine Finger Paints doesn't turn out to be the artistic, humanitarian haven you were hoping for.

The Job Interview in Three Steps

While the moment of The Job Interview looms large in our cultural imagination, negotiating a job offer is usually a process that occurs over several conversations rather than in a single interview. We break the negotiation of a job offer into three distinct parts. Sometimes these parts happen in quick succession, while in other situations they might be spread out over a long period of time.

1. Getting in the room—landing the interview from a target decision maker
2. Evaluating the fit—evaluating how well a job opportunity or collaboration meets your interests and those of your potential employer
3. Negotiating the offer—defining the terms of your future working relationship, or gracefully deciding not to work together

Breaking these Phase 3 negotiations into distinct parts is useful because you need slightly different negotiation strategies for each part.

Getting in the Room

In this advanced stage of the job hunt, your connectors or colleagues can often get you a direct line to a decision maker, or they can help you get close enough that you can easily establish communication. You've accumulated lots of access capital, so it should be no surprise if getting access to decision makers isn't a huge hurdle at this stage. If you're already in, you're already in! Set up the meeting and skip down to "Evaluating the Fit" below.

But in many situations, depending on the nature of your target opportunities and your good (or not so good) fortune with connectors and work opportunities thus far, you'll have to do some more work. You might need to be creative to get in the room with decision makers so you can make your case and negotiate for an ideal role. Maybe there is no direct line of communication to a target decision maker because there's an administrative firewall between them and you—an online application process, organizational bureaucracy, or a bevy of assistants. You may need to grapple with a human resources officer or some other form of gatekeeper to get in the room with the primary decision maker. You may have one gatekeeper or a whole series of them. For instance, some companies have a policy not to interview anyone who does not meet with a recruiter or have an initial meeting with an internal hiring agent first. Faced with this possibility, your first, perfectly natural question might be, "Can I bypass the gatekeepers?"

In some situations policies are firm, and anyone trying to get around them may be swiftly turned away. A friend of Tad's researched and queried connectors to find the hidden decision maker for a job posted on an employment website. He sent his résumé and cover letter directly to the decision maker for the posting. The response he got was a form letter from human resources stating the company's policy that all applications must go through the online submission process. His options were to go through the dictated online process, look to his connectors to try to get access another way, or contact the decision maker in some other, more creative fashion—for instance, meeting the decision maker at a conference.

If you can't go around the process, you want to find out who the primary gatekeeper is and view them as a decision maker, because for now they are. And you have to make a pitch to the gatekeeper based on *their* interests. Your goal in this interim negotiation is to get access to the ultimate decision maker. Fortunately, gatekeepers are often easier to reach than the decision makers they guard. You can email or call them, or sometimes (but rarely these days) you can drop into the office in person and try to meet with them. In cases where even the gatekeepers are hard to reach, go back and consult with your connectors—or a new connector—for advice on how to crack this organizational puzzle.

Generally speaking, if you can meet a gatekeeper's interests, they will be open to allowing you access to the decision maker. By showing that you understand what is important to them and not just bombarding them with explanations of how you fit the job description, you will stand out as someone able to identify and speak to interests.

If bypassing gatekeepers is possible and isn't viewed as a major faux pas, great—you are effectively in the same position as if there were no gatekeepers. You can look for opportunities to access the decision maker directly. You can find out what conferences they attend and where they will be speaking, cold-call during off hours, or show up at their office. If you do get this sort of impromptu access to them, you want to at least pique their curiosity.

For a particularly dramatic example: A young man famously approached Steve Jobs in a parking lot out of the blue, asking if they could meet. Jobs tried to wave him off, but the young man said, "No, please, just take a look at this," holding up his open laptop. Glimpsing the screen, Jobs quickly realized the potential of the young man's idea and agreed to meet with him. The man had invented the first iteration of the dock—now a standard of the Apple operating system display.[*]

A more everyday example comes from one of Tad's clients, who had been pursuing an executive placement. It was a joint industry/government/academic effort to develop software for the next generation of manufacturing in the United States, with an emphasis on Department of Defense suppliers. He had what seemed like very productive talks with a human resources agent for a few weeks when all of a sudden his HR contact stopped taking his calls or returning his emails.

[*] Walter Isaacson, *Steve Jobs* (New York: Simon & Schuster, 2011), 477.

TAD: After two weeks of this silence, Carston and I discussed the possibility of him approaching the managing director directly at a talk he was giving downtown. It was possible that the decision maker had no idea that Carston was interested or even existed. Carston and I discussed what the managing director's motivations and interests might be, and how to approach him. Carston had already spoken to connectors and knew that the director wanted to fill the post as quickly as possible with someone who had an industry background, which Carston did. The director was also an academic who was somewhat introverted, intellectual, and focused on people's depth and character, and who cared deeply about respect.

Carston and I discussed many options for an approach, from bold and abrupt—"Hi, I'm your next COO!"—to lower intensity: "Hello, my name is Carston, and I just wanted to introduce myself since I've been working with HR on the open COO role. I enjoyed your talk and wanted to meet you." Based on what he knew about the director's interests, Carston chose the latter approach, which gave the director a choice: between starting a conversation and just shaking hands and moving on. When Carston approached him, the director asked him to sit down and talk. Shortly thereafter HR resumed contact with Carston as a candidate for the open COO role.

No matter how you find a way to get in the same room—or parking lot—with the decision makers, you will have to make an ask. Whether it's done in person, by phone, email, or letter, you're asking for a meeting. If you have enough access capital, you stand a good chance of having them agree to meet with you. If you don't, you have to make a pitch to their interests. Show that you understand what they're looking for and have an idea that is worth their time. Your opening contact with the decision maker should address their specific interests, and how working with you would meet their interests. You're looking to communicate in a credible way: "If you meet with me, I can show you how I'll help you achieve what's important to you."

Be aware that if you are making a pitch to get in the room, what you're asking for is likely to be one of two things.

1. An interview for an existing job. You are responding to a job posting, or there is an open role you're aware of although there is no official posting. Maybe a connector told you about a friend who is looking for someone, or you read in the paper that a major retailer is opening a new store in your area, but they haven't officially posted jobs yet. Almost half of all jobs are never advertised publicly, so you're likely to be in the latter situation at some point.

2. A meeting to create a job or collaboration. You are ignoring that there is no posting and no specific opportunity that you know of. But you do know enough about a company and its mission that you see a potential opportunity they are missing and you want to be the person to launch it. Or, even better, you know of an initiative that someone at the company is interested in but doesn't have time to push it forward themselves—that's where you come in.

In either of these scenarios, the process of getting in the room is basically the same; what changes is how you open the ask. If there is an open job, they will already understand why you are contacting them. If nothing is open, you'll have to justify your contacting them with a pitch that demonstrates your informed ideas about what they need or could stand to gain.

Evaluating the Fit

So you're in the room. Now what?

When interviewing, aim to establish fit rather than simply projecting "Please pick me!" Can they meet your interests, and can you meet theirs? Is there fit? Making fit the object of conversation will make you come across as confident, professional, and purposeful, and you'll avoid projecting an air of desperation: "I'll be whatever you want me to be!"

It is tempting to go into the interview willing to say whatever it takes to get the job. But your potential employer may view your apparent eagerness to adapt as confusing and possibly disingenuous. If you are not consistent in how you present yourself, the decision maker may not be able to imagine what type of employee they would be hiring by choosing you. You're not all things. No one is. And by showing that fit and interests are your priorities, you will come across as genuine, authentic, focused, and unique.

For you, fit shouldn't mean merely that they are a cool company or that they have an incredible campus or are offering a huge salary. The way their offer meets the whole range of things that are important to you is what should define fit. Ask yourself, "Is what they want in a top-performing employee what I want to be doing?" Beyond your work responsibilities, consider how the work culture and environment line up with what you want. Is the team you will be working with one that *you* would choose? Are the salary range and benefits going to meet your key need for financial security? If you have no alternatives, and therefore little negotiating power, you may be required to hold the level of fit to a lower standard: "Can I do what they want, even though it is not what I would choose to do? Can I make do?" Again, this is why taking the time to seek good alternatives is so important.

In practical terms, your focus should be to turn the interview into a two-way conversation instead of just their questions and your answers. If this is truly a conversation about fit, they are interviewing you and you are interviewing them. Many interviews will have a set structure that doesn't give you much flexibility. Others will allow you to influence the conversation's flow. Ideally, you would start out framing the conversation around fit and then ask them questions about what they are looking for as early in the conversation as you can. This is the start of turning the interview into a two-way conversation. Ask them about their interests, beyond just the job description.

- What are the major needs of your team right now?
- What are your goals for the next year?

- What do you want to be known for in this company, and how do you think I might fit in with that vision?

You will have to use your judgment about how to raise these questions in an interview. In very formal interviews, there is often a point toward the end when the interviewer asks if you have any questions for them. As discussed in previous chapters, when inquiring about interests, one of the best ways to focus your thinking is to attempt to note, either mentally or in writing, the interests that are most important to them. Once you have what you believe to be a full list, you can reflect it back to the decision maker: "So it sounds like you're looking for someone who can offer X, Y, and Z. If you found someone who met all of these interests, is there anything else you would want?"

After inquiring about their interests, take some time to share yours: "The reason I'm interested in this job is that it meets my professional goals for deepening my management experience in the transportation sector. And for me personally, this job aligns with my desire to be based in the Baltimore area and to have the opportunity to work on a team that shares my commitment to public service." By including your interests in the conversation, you can prime the decision maker to think about creative ways to meet your interests.

Once your interests and theirs are out on the table and the fit potential is clear, it's time to move to options for how your working relationship might look. In the case of well-defined, formal roles, the options will be limited. In cases where you are pitching an idea to an employer, or where the job is still in the early stages of development, you will have much more space for creativity. In either case, your purpose is the same: to find ways to make the proposal on the table more attractive for one or both of you without making either worse off.

Your goal in generating options is to work together to push your potential for mutual value. You can ask, "What could we do to make this opportunity better for both of us?" Or you can alternate between focusing on them and focusing on you: "How can I go beyond the job description for your company?" Then discuss how working at the company could meet one of your interests. Another way to engage the conversation around creating value is to explore ideal scenarios without appearing overly presumptuous—you're still conveying interests, after all, not making demands. Ask them what the perfect arrangement with a new hire or contractor would look like, and share what your ideal terms and working relationship would look like.

If there is an obvious fit, you and the decision maker will end up creating a package of options that works best for both of you. Your challenge will be to keep thinking creatively even once the deal looks good to both of you. A few extra minutes of brainstorming can make the difference between a satisfactory deal and an amazing one. After laying out a first proposal, add another and ask for their feedback to test whether you're both truly on the same page.

> *JUSTIN:* Once I was far enough into my Phase 3 that I was consistently getting hired to teach conflict management trainings, I negotiated with a decision maker about the possibility of co-leading a corporate negotiation training. We reached an agreement for a fair rate and developed a plan for me to learn the needed material. We were both happy with the deal. Still, we took a few extra minutes to see if there were any other ways we could meet each other's interests. At that time I had an interest in helping colleagues get exposure to negotiation training, and the decision maker had an interest in focusing on organizational leadership rather than devoting time and energy to leading a popular open enrollment class that he usually taught. Given these interests, we decided that I could also teach his open enrollment course at a reduced rate in exchange for allowing two of my colleagues to attend the course for free. Adding the extra people to the course cost him nothing and was of great value to me. Teaching the course at a reduced rate was a relatively minimal cost for me and of great value to the decision maker as it solved his scheduling dilemma and saved him money.

Once you've generated options, discovered a collaborative arrangement that you can both agree to, and done all you can to make the proposal better, you will have to evaluate and negotiate the offer's details.

Negotiating the Offer

The fact that you're negotiating an offer means you found a clear and compelling fit between your interests and the decision maker's—congratulations! Now you have an opportunity to further expand the pie and claim your fair share. "Expanding the pie" is a phrase used often in the negotiation field that means making the outcome better for both of you—making a good deal even better by figuring out if it's possible to meet *even more* of the interests on the table.

Note that there are numerous books that describe competitive, haggle-based salary negotiation. We focus here on a collaborative approach to negotiating compensation. There is certainly value in what you can learn about bargaining in other books. At the same time, the discussion below will help you utilize the concepts from previous chapters that we hope you are now practicing to build value as you work through compensation options with potential employers.

Preparation

During your negotiations around fit, you'll have already taken a serious look at the interests and options on the table. Now, to start the conversation about salary, for instance, you'll need to prepare at least one additional negotiation element: objective standards, which will help you determine what is the most favorable and fair outcome.

The term *objective standards* refers to standard practices and trends that govern your field and the economy at large. These might be based on laws, well-accepted tradition, market analysis, or other recognized factors. To determine what would be a fair salary, you can start your research online. You can compare similar jobs at other companies by looking through websites like the Bureau of

Labor Statistics Wage Data, PayScale, or Glassdoor. These websites are especially helpful if you're doing a popular, formalized job that many other people also do. Some jobs, particularly niche jobs or roles in fledgling fields, don't have easily accessible salary information available online. In that case, you'll need to turn to your network of connectors to ask what they believe would be fair based on their perception of the market combined with your experience level.

You'll want to do good research on rates, salaries, and benefits of people in comparable roles or on comparable projects. The better your research, the more convincing it will be to the decision maker. You are much more likely to be able to influence a potential employer or client to pay your desired salary if you are able to persuade them that the amount is fair and justified by objective standards rather than by your feelings about how much you *think* you should earn. Do your homework.

After researching objective standards, prepare your alternatives. As discussed above, the better your alternatives to taking this offer, the more power you will have within the negotiation to ask for what you are worth. Before you enter into the negotiation, you need to know what your alternatives are in detail. For each other offer (or staying in your current role), take the time to summarize the salary, equity package, health coverage, vacation time, and other benefits or considerations. Then ask yourself, "If the offer I'm about to negotiate falls through, which is my best alternative for meeting my interests?" Knowing your best alternative, and its details, simplifies making a comparison to the offer you are about to negotiate.

You also need to anticipate what their alternatives are. Your connectors may provide you with information, research may give you insight, or you may have to speculate. What would they do if they decided not to hire you? How do you compare to their alternatives? What can you do to make yourself more appealing than their alternatives, and still meet your own interests?

At the end of your preparation process, you should have four tools:

1. A list of your interests and the decision maker's interests
2. An outline of the options proposed, and ideas for how to make these options more attractive for each of you
3. A thorough and persuasive set of objective standards
4. An identified—and improved, if possible—best alternative to this offer

With those in hand, you are ready to sit down with the decision maker to negotiate your offer.

The Negotiation

The best way to start a negotiation around an offer is with appreciation and a strong collaborative opening. Discussing salary or payment can be as stressful for employers and clients as it can be for you. Under this kind of stress many people will default to a competitive mindset that will make it hard for you to find creative ways to make the deal better and also make it harder for you to persuade them to pay you more than the minimum.

Always start by thanking the potential employer for the offer, even if you don't like it. They chose you! They gave you an offer to work there! Acknowledge that first and foremost. Then, send a collaborative signal early in the conversation, making sure that it's clear and low-cost. Try giving the employer or client something they want up front. Only give things that are not a major sacrifice for you. Saying, "I am so excited about this job that I'd do it for $10 an hour," would probably get your *relationship* off to a great start, but that could be a very costly way to get your dream job. Instead of offering to work for a lower salary, you could open with offering something they need that you can easily do: "Thank you for the offer. Let me start off by saying that it is my understanding that you are hoping to fill this posting quickly. If we come to an agreement that works for both of us, I am happy to be flexible on the start date. I could even start this afternoon." The key is that you start the conversation by doing something to put you both on the same side of the negotiation, as long as it does not involve giving up something that's important to you. The lowest-cost way to do this is simply to express your appreciation for being selected and excitement about the opportunity's potential.

After demonstrating your preference for collaborating, the next step is to review both your interests and theirs and make sure there is no benefit to either of you that you failed to see in your fit conversation. In that conversation you started expanding the pie then, addressing things like your responsibilities and potential contributions, the people you will work, with, and your expected advancement.

Here you can expand the pie further by revisiting those topics and focusing on compensation options, such as salary, benefits, vacation, equipment to complete work, stock options, moving expenses, remote work options, professional development courses, expenses, or pay for travel time. For example, if you would benefit from the flexibility of being able to take a course at a local university that will improve your work product, now would be the time to inquire about whether shifting your hours to allow for that would work for your decision maker. After clarifying the interests you've already mentioned, check in to see if there is anything you could do to make the offer better for either of you: "Is there anything that would make hiring me more attractive for you?" or "One thing that occurred to me since our last conversation that might make my working here better for both of us would be . . ."

One common mistake is to dive right into the conversation about salary before talking about how you could make the offer better in creative ways. How much money it will take for you to say yes will depend on what goes into the whole package of the offer. If the conversation about salary comes after you and your potential employer or client have explored ways to make the offer better, then it will be easier to establish an appropriate salary given the entire context of the offer. A conversation about salary is focused on scarcity—a fixed pie that can't be expanded—and how to divide it: how much you get and they give up.

William Ury explains in *Getting Past No* that "[e]ffective negotiators do not just divvy up a fixed pie. They first explore how to expand the pie."* Once you get into the conversation about pay, it is difficult to go back to discussing creative options.

When it comes to negotiating for salary and benefits, generally speaking, the more ambitious you are in what you ask for, the more you will get. Still, people tend to accept the salary they are offered as is. Research shows that women are especially reluctant to ask for a salary higher than what is offered. Research *also* supports that most people—of any gender—who ask for a higher salary do succeed in getting more than what was initially offered. For this reason, it is important to research what would be a fair agreement based on objective standards, and then consider asking for the higher end of the fair range if they do not offer it to you.

The only time to consider not negotiating an offer is when connectors, anecdotes, or policies indicate that it will seriously jeopardize the opportunity. We want you to go into the conversation about salary with the goal of being paid an ambitious and fair salary. Sadly, that is not always what the employer will offer you right off the bat. You are not trying to wring as much as you can get out of the employer, but we also don't want you to abandon your expectations in order to get hired. Again, finding the right balance is where objective standards come into play.

Some of the time, even when you anchor your salary expectations at the high end of fair, the decision maker will simply accept your offer. And sometimes you might experience resistance and pushback when negotiating. Employers often present offers in ways that discourage negotiation. Potential employers try to avoid negotiating by:

- Not giving you an obvious opening to negotiate.
- Getting you to agree to a number early in the hiring process.
- Basing an offer on what you had been making previously.

---

* William Ury, *Getting Past No: Negotiating in Difficult Situations* (New York: Bantam, 1991), 19.

- Telling you that they'll make up for a low salary with a great benefits package.
- Saying there's no room for additional money now while alluding to increases down the road.*

Try to frame your negotiation as an exploratory conversation with the decision maker about what is fair. To do this, speak from a place of fact and objectivity versus emotion and mere belief. When you receive an offer, instead of saying, "Well, I think I'm worth 15 percent more," use your research and your alternatives to say something like, "PayScale says that the average salary for this type of job here in Chicago is 15 percent higher than what you are offering. I want to make sure that we come to an agreement that is fair. I think it would be reasonable to expect at least the average salary for this kind of role. What do you think?" Even when leading with objective standards, be aware that you may have to compare notes with the decision maker. Their take on the market may be different from yours, which is why it's so important that you take the time to research salary standards from multiple sources.

With objective standards on the table, you can now get into the details of creating a package of terms for employment that is specific and concrete. The best way to do this is to start putting together ideas for terms but to make clear that nothing is decided until everything is decided. In other words, you might agree to a lower starting salary if they agree to an extra two weeks of vacation. If the employer comes back and says they can only offer one extra week of vacation, then the salary proposal is up for renegotiation. A major mistake in multi-issue negotiations of this kind is to agree on terms one at a time. This eliminates the possibility of making shifts like this, and it can lock you into something unfavorable and leave you without leverage in another area that's important to you.

---

* Alison Green, "5 Ways Employers Discourage You from Negotiating Salary," *US News & World Report*, February 2, 2015, http://money.usnews.com/money /blogs/outside-voices-careers/2015/02/02/5-ways-employers-discourage-you-from-negotiating-salary?src=usn_tw.

Do not commit to anything until you agree to everything. This leaves you flexibility to come back to items that you have discussed but not yet committed to, which can help prevent impasse as you address new items. For example, at the end of the negotiation, if the employer comes back to you with the "bad news from his boss" that they can't actually offer you the amount of vacation you wanted, leaving the whole deal open until the end allows you to say, "That's too bad. I'm ready to commit to the terms we discussed previously. If we have to decrease the vacation time, then let's look at what else we could change to make this offer equal to the one we had on the table before."

If it turns out that the best terms the employer is willing to offer leave you worse off than you would be with your best alternative, then you have two options. One is to turn down the offer and go to your best alternative. The second is to attempt to use your alternative as leverage to get the decision maker to offer you a better deal. Your leverage will stem from how much they need to hire you—either because you are such a good fit or because their candidate pool is not ideal. When sharing your alternatives, do your best to keep them from coming across as threatening or aggressive. Threats evoke strong emotional reactions, and you want to keep the conversation cool-headed.

In the spirit of collaboration, you can present your alternative by framing it as asking for their help: "Because of your company's culture and leadership in the industry, I really want to find a way to work here. At the same time, it is important to me to accept an offer that maximizes my compensation. I have an offer from Other Company, Inc., for $70,000 with similar benefits to your offer. I'm struggling with what to do since you have offered me a salary of $60,000. What's the best way to approach this?" If they have no answer except, "Just take our offer," you can ask, "What flexibility do you have to increase either the salary offer or another part of the benefits package, and how can I help you justify offering me higher compensation?" By presenting your alternative as a shared challenge, you avoid the risk of triggering a defensive response.

Your last step in this negotiation, assuming that the final offer from the decision maker is more attractive than your alternatives, is to make sure the agreement will hold up. When you have put together a package that works for both of you, you have to consider what could go wrong with it.

One set of questions you want to ask falls into the category of what Harvard professors Michael Watkins and Max Bazerman call "predictable surprises."* While preparing for your negotiation, take a few minutes on your own to identify what might go wrong and what might go better than expected. You should bring up these predictable surprises toward the end of your negotiation with the decision maker—once you've gotten close to agreeing on a package that works for both of you, but before you commit to a final agreement. For example: What if you get sick while on deployment abroad and you can't finish the project? What if you decide to attend graduate school? What if your boss doesn't have time to train you as you both expected? What if the client portfolio you are handling outperforms the firm average by more than 50 percent, which is what you achieved at your last job? For those predictable surprises that seem likely enough to occur, take the time to talk about options for terms you may need to add to the agreement.

In addition, you want to make sure that all of the terms you have agreed upon are clear, that you know how they will be executed, and that both you and the decision maker agree on them in the same way. If, for example, you are counting on using the signing bonus to pay part of the down payment on a home you are closing on next week and the employer's practice is to not pay out the signing bonuses until the first day on the job, which will not be for another three months, then you have a problem. Make sure you ask all of the who, what, when, where, and how questions about the various elements of the agreement before signing. With those additions, now you're done!

* Max H. Bazerman and Michael D. Watrkins, *Predictable Surprises: The Disasters You Should Have Seen Coming and How to Prevent Them* (Boston: Harvard Business School, 2008).

PHASE 4

Building Greater Fulfillment

All Three Conversations

10

The Vision of You—Fulfilled

If you have Phase 3 well in hand, you've been doing work that you love for a while, you're good at it, and people know it. You have colleagues, clients, and peers who recognize and value what you do. By conventional standards, you've made it. Congratulations! That is definitely worth celebrating! *And* it's an opportunity for you to ask, "What's next?" It's time to start examining whether you are also living a fully satisfying lifestyle and impacting the world in a way that aligns with the legacy you want to have.

In the previous three phases, the answer to "What's next?" was somewhat narrower. In Phase 1 the answer was "Get clear on my direction." In Phase 2 it was "Gain access to my field." In Phase 3 it was "Get work I love and excel at it." The next step here in Phase 4 requires some fresh soul-searching. You're now asking, "What does *fulfillment* look like for me?" As we define it, fulfillment has two basic, overlapping elements: the impact you want to have on the world and the lifestyle you want to maintain.

Your impact interests will be unique to your situation and ambitions. Maybe you want to improve the treatment of refugees in your country, or bring joy and a sympathetic ear to the patrons of the restaurant where you work. Perhaps you want to start affordable farmers markets in areas where access to quality food is limited, or ensure that your children can graduate from college without unmanageable debt, or share your valuable accounting skills with local small businesses.

Your lifestyle is about what your day-to-day life is actually like—its pace, rhythm, and texture. How and with whom you spend your time, how you work, socialize, exercise, study, interact with those close to you, and continue to grow as a person. As with impact, everyone's lifestyle interests will look different. Yours might include having a boss who will let you leave early to see your seventh grader triumph in the spelling bee, or a hobby that gets you up in time to enjoy the sunrise every day, or a job that allows you to speak in your first language. You might prioritize a lifestyle that allows you to work remotely while you care for aging parents. Or maybe you're a brilliant salesperson and you need to spend more time interacting with clients and patrons and less time fretting about the logistics side of your business.

When you're riding high in Phase 3, it's time to start taking a bolder look at the impact you want to make in the world and at the same time, taking a strong stand for yourself—for your own happiness and well-being. Phase 4, Building Greater Fulfillment, is about taking care of yourself and living out your dreams by (1) developing a vision of what fulfillment looks like for you and (2) gathering an amazing team of collaborators and supporters to make that vision a reality.

For some, finding fulfillment in Phase 4 may require a dramatic career change. That would mean a return to earlier phases and building new networks and access capital. For others, Phase 4 fulfillment will just mean making adjustments to the career path they're already on. Whichever case applies to you, you'll need a group of collaborators to support you in achieving your lifestyle and impact interests. This is a critical aspect of Phase 4 that requires a negotiation approach.

No matter what your vision for achieving fulfillment, pursuing it all on your own is not an option: involving others in your Phase 4 plans early is crucial to avoiding false starts or just flat-out inaction. So, it makes sense that much of your work now will be focused on building the team that will help you bring your lifestyle and impact interests to fruition. The only part of this phase that comes from you and you alone is this opening self-negotiation, which we call "re-visioning." In Phase 1 you spent a lot of time negotiating with yourself to decide on a vision for your career. In Phase 4, you are now an established professional and your vision for the rest of your career is probably different from what you imagined in previous phases. As you enter Phase 4, it's time to zoom out and take a bird's-eye view of your Interest Profile to make sure you're meeting your larger fulfillment interests—lifestyle and impact interests—that you might not have had the luxury to pursue earlier in your career.

Dan, a friend of the authors, had built a career in media that met many of his interests. When he found himself getting comfortable in Phase 3, he spent some time reexamining his Interest Profile and discovered there were some interests that weren't being met in his current work setup. This self-negotiation propelled him into a Phase 4 process of restructuring his work life to better meet his fulfillment interests.

Dan was a successful executive at a thriving media company he had founded that had grown tremendously in just four years. He believed that his current job was meeting most of his career interests: he was providing for his family, starting projects that allowed him to be creative, pushing the limits in an industry he loved, and spending his days building teams and thinking critically. He was caught up in the work, and there were a lot of elements of it he loved. However, every now and then he noticed that his career had lost some of the thrill it used to have, and he didn't know why. So he took some time off to think. He knew he still wanted challenging work, but didn't know what else that could look like.

By taking time to intentionally reexamine his vision for what he wanted moving forward, Dan was finally able to put his finger on some interests that weren't being met and were causing him to feel unfulfilled. It turned out that Dan's existing list of career interests didn't encompass his newly emerging impact and lifestyle interests. As he negotiated with himself at the beginning of Phase 4, he uncovered a whole host of new interests: He wanted to be home in time to say goodnight to his three kids, to feel like he was leaving a meaningful mark on the world, and to immerse himself in the math that had inspired him to study engineering in college.

Capturing these new lifestyle and impact interests was a critical first step for Dan's pursuit of a Phase 4 vision. What he did next is the early work of negotiating with Phase 4 connectors: he began sharing his list of updated interests with family, friends, and colleagues. A connector conversation with his sister led to a surprising suggestion—surprising to Dan, at least—try teaching. And that's what he ultimately did. He wasn't the only one who was surprised. Many people in his life were shocked that he would sell his company and transition to teaching. But the more he had thought about it and learned about it from people who shared with him what it was like and how to get into it, the more he realized that teaching was a great option for him.

Through many conversations, Dan did the challenging and fruitful work of honing his vision and assembling a team of people to help him achieve his Phase 4 vision: to teach high school mathematics. He consulted his sister, who holds a prominent position in education in Boston, and spoke with many connectors he'd built relationships with in Phase 2. By doing this, he found a lot of overlap with the work he did at his company. Teaching was just a new style of doing presentations—one that resonated with him more at that point in his life. He was motivated by his own memories of how hard high school was, and he wanted to be one of the people who gets kids excited about something. He realized that in addition to teaching geometry and precalculus, he wanted to teach students to be lifelong learners by showing them the value in that. And being a teacher would allow him to better match his schedule to his kids' schedules, so he could spend more time with them.

Like Dan, you might have important, emerging interests that are subtly going unmet. Often, as in Dan's case, our jobs appear to be meeting our interests, but there might still be a sense of something missing. Without doing the important reflection work of negotiating with yourself in Phase 4, this misalignment can go on for years. It is often tempting just to leave well enough alone, even if you know your work life isn't really serving you anymore. Sometimes you can get stuck in a rut if you're evaluating your life based on previous interests that no longer drive you as they once did, rather than by your current interests. For many people, it is simply easier to keep doing something that was at some point the epitome of doing the work you love. No matter the justification, stasis can be extremely tempting, which is why your Phase 4 negotiation with yourself is an important checkpoint to see if there are adjustments you can make to better meet your current lifestyle and impact interests.

Dan made a bold move to satisfy his impact and lifestyle interests. He feels enthusiastic and excited about his work again, he is nourishing and challenging his mathematical mind, and he has made his family his central focus. None of this would have been possible if he had not first allowed himself to think about what parts of his life were no longer working, and then taken time to re-vision what had become important to him.

Re-visioning Beyond the Work You Love

It's easy to find a million reasons not to negotiate with yourself for your ideal lifestyle or impact. Many professionals have no process for stepping back and taking stock of their shifting interests and desires, and so they eventually lose sight of whether they are actually living and working in a way that feels fulfilling. As a consequence, many careers drift at the whim of circumstance and short-term thinking. If avoiding this kind of drift is important to you, taking time to step back and envision your trajectory is critical once you have the work of Phase 3 behind you.

To pursue fulfillment in your life, you have to clarify and prioritize your interests so that you can set your sights on a vision of fulfillment, that is, a target situation: an ideal picture of a work-life balance that convincingly meets your impact and lifestyle interests.

That target doesn't need to have an incredible amount of detail at this point, but it does need to capture your imagination: Maybe you want to found a joint program in space art between MIT and the University of Hong Kong, or run a successful chain of fitness facilities whose machines feed power into the electricity grid, or maybe you want to grow a network of maker fairs that help bring skills and technology to underserved communities. These are visions more than action plans, and they are starting points as much as horizons. But how to get there?

Re-Visioning: EXERCISE 5

We find that without taking time to do intentional re-visioning, most people can get stuck in the inertia of doing what they are already good at. To get the most out of intentional re-visioning, you will want to ensure that you hold some dedicated time for reflection. This exercise will give structure to the re-visioning process. For this one, it's essential to read through the full set of instructions and Worksheet 5 before blocking out the time, so you can anticipate your preparation needs and allocate enough time to reflect while you're doing the exercise.

We encourage you to create extra space in your life for some positive ruminating in the weeks or days directly preceding your structured reflection exercise. This type of mind-clearing contemplation can take many forms, and it is most important that you find a method that works well for you. For Justin, this means extracting himself from his daily environments and retreating into nature because he finds it easier to open his mind away from the office. Before his re-visioning exercise, he went hiking for two days in the White Mountains. Tad made space for open-ended reflection by taking long walks with his dog and going to work at the office very early in the morning to reflect in a quiet space before the demands of the day took over. Carly spends time reflecting during everyday activities like commuting or cooking, and also by taking the time to talk through their reflections in therapy and with close friends.

EXERCISE 5 WORKSHEET

RE-VISIONING

Scan QR Code or visit
findingajobthatlovesyouback.com
for the free downloadable worksheet

PURPOSE:	To create space for you to reflect on how well your current life fulfills your impact and lifestyle interests, and to generate ideas for making adjustments that would allow you to meet any unmet interests
RESULT:	A prioritized list of interests for the life you want to lead and some ideas for how you might meet them
TIME:	Two to three 2-hour blocks
PREPARATION:	A journal, notebook, laptop, or whatever works best for helping you organize your thoughts and notes
INSTRUCTIONS:	Pages 220–30

PART 1
APPRECIATIVE INQUIRY

PART 2
PRIORITIZATION

PART 3
VISIONING

Where and how you do your most expansive thinking is ultimately a personal preference. The important thing is that you do this as preparation for your re-visioning exercise.

When you finally do sit down to do the exercise, you'll have a few ideas marinating. How and where you do the exercise is up to you. It could be an afternoon spent with a journal and a cup of tea in a park or with a large whiteboard in a conference room, or it could be sitting at a lookout in the mountains, on a rooftop, or at a bed and breakfast out of town. What matters is that you find a distraction-free environment. The time you should hold for this exercise will depend on how you think and process ideas. We have found that two to three two-hour blocks can work well for working through the exercise without getting exhausted. If you have the space and energy for it, though, you could probably work through much of the thinking in half a day of focused work.

One last thing: Although the questions you need to answer when negotiating with yourself in Phase 4 are personal, this is work that can also be done with another person or in a group if you are better served by having other minds working alongside yours. So long as your companions respect the process and what you're trying to achieve, go ahead and make it social. Here goes!

The three parts of this exercise—appreciative inquiry, prioritization, and visioning—will help you identify and organize your lifestyle and impact interests to create an inspiring, future-focused vision for what your work life could be. The appreciative inquiry will help you establish a prioritized list of interests that relate to the kind of impact you want to have in the world and the lifestyle you hope to have.

For this exercise we recommend that you use a journal, notebook, or laptop—or a combination—since it can take some time to complete the exercise and you want to have your notes in a place where you will not lose them.

From our experience of coaching re-visioning work, we recommend blocking out some uninterrupted time to think, reflect, and write and then stepping away for a few days or even weeks to let what you reflected percolate. When you feel ready, block out another hour or two to return to the exercise wherever you left off.

It can be helpful to talk through some of these questions with trusted friends and mentors between journaling sessions too. We recommend that you hold time to do the exercises themselves on your own first.

Part 1: Appreciative Inquiry

David Cooperrider and Suresh Srivastva developed the appreciative inquiry process in the late 1980s, and we recommend it for its elegant simplicity and focus on the future and on the positive. It is meant to focus on what is working well in your career and life so far. The formula is simple: recognize and carry forward what interests are already working for you and consider what interests you want to meet in the future that are not currently being met. During the subsequent steps of the exercise, you will take the pieces of your appreciative inquiry and order them according to importance. This sorting and prioritizing of interests and goals makes it easier to sketch out the beginnings of a vision of fulfillment—a Phase 4 target—that you can build toward.

To begin, answer each of the following four questions, using a fresh page for each question so that you have enough space to add to and change your lists as needed.

Current Appreciation

1. What impact am I having on my industry, company, community, friends, family, and even myself? What in my current work and life is already having the kind of impact I want to have in the world?
2. Which of my interests are being met by my current lifestyle?

Future Desires

1. What impact interests do I want to be met going forward?

2. What lifestyle interests do I want to be met in the future?

Your list of responses from questions 1 and 2, taken together, should give you a clear picture of what is working for you and what you want to carry forward. For your answers to questions 3 and 4, it can be helpful to look back at the interests behind the ideas you generated during your Phase 1 Thinking Expansively exercise, when you asked yourself what you would do if you had infinite resources, were free from other people's judgment, or could not fail. Bring this same kind of expansive thinking and ambition into your answers to these questions. Focus on what motivations and aspirations you want for the future but don't already have, so that you're not duplicating the lists from 1 and 2.

As you answer the future-oriented questions, we encourage you to come up with as many interests as you can. Some ideas may contradict each other or be mutually exclusive. That's okay. Soon you will prioritize and sort out which are most important to your emerging vision of fulfillment. For now, just create as robust a list as you can.

Because it is often easier to think in terms of options than interests, feel free to answer these questions in a more concrete way— writing what you think you actually want to do—and then work backward to find the interests. In the example below, you will see in parentheses the options that came to mind for Justin when completing the exercise and then also the interest that the options meet. By distilling the initial concrete options into interests, many more, and often better, options will come to light for your vision. Here is what this might look like in practice based on Justin's experience.

Justin entered Phase 4 after having worked for several years as a mediator and negotiation trainer. He and a business partner had started a negotiation and conflict resolution consulting firm. As the company started running more smoothly, they were no longer scrambling to answer the question "What does it take to do this job well?" but rather "What type of work do we want to focus on and who are our ideal clients?" This question of company direction actually prompted bigger questions for Justin as an individual, which led him to work through an appreciative inquiry process. Here are some selections from the lists he came up with.

1. Interests being met by the impact I am having on my industry, firm, community, friends, family, and even myself

- Impacting decision makers involved in climate change and other social justice and sustainability challenges (Option: work with organizations and activists who are trying to find intelligent answers)
- Enabling lasting change in the communication skills and behavior of my university students and professional training course participants (Option: explicit teaching about behavior change in each course)
- Working with colleagues I respect and can learn from (Option: work with the team of Tad, Carly, and others)

2. Interests being met by my current lifestyle

- Having a flexible schedule and no geographic constraints (Option: work remotely)
- Exercising and going dancing often (Option: run, gym membership, and Cuban salsa team)
- Having a structure that enforces my work-life balance (Option: have a colleague manage my calendar)

3. Impact interests I want to be met going forward

- Increasing the percentage of our clients who are companies or nonprofits working on social justice, sustainability, and responsible natural resource management (Option: develop relationship with organizations that can give us the lay of the land and help us develop these relationships)
- Spreading the skills we teach (Option: make video content about negotiation and behavior change)
- Scaling up the work we do without compromising quality (Option: build teams of trainers and create an excellent archive of written and audio resources for new trainers)

4. Lifestyle interests I want to meet in the future
- Meditating and stretching every day (Option: schedule a consistent time daily for these activities)
- Ensuring that the pace of my life at home (that is, when not traveling for work) feels relaxed and manageable (Options: turn internet off at home and ask the colleague that manages my calendar to help enforce that time off is time off)
- Climbing mountains! (Options: Denali in Alaska and Chimborazo in Ecuador)

Justin generated this list of current appreciations and future desires over several sessions, refining, tweaking, and adding as he went. Once you have your own list of reflections on what has worked for you in the past and what you would like in the future, you will be ready to bring focus to your next steps.

Part 2: Prioritization

At this point, your lists will probably be long and varied. To craft a clear vision that captures what is most important to you, you'll need to prioritize your interests by grouping them into three categories: must have, should have, and nice to have. This way you know where to focus your attention.

On a new page, create a Prioritization Table that looks something like this:

	Must Have	Should Have	Nice to Have
Impact			
Lifestyle			

Review each item from the four lists you created during your appreciative inquiry and place each one accordingly. As you transfer items over from the future-focused appreciative inquiry lists, place a star next to them to indicate if they are *not yet* being met.

There are a few things to look out for as you prioritize. First, not everything can be a must-have. It can be tempting to have all your dreams be the most important, but that will dilute your focus. Try to set yourself a limit. For example, you can decide to give yourself at most two must-haves and three should-haves in each category. Second, it's possible that something important slipped your mind in the first pass. Once you've completed a first draft of your priorities, look to see if anything is missing. Review your must-haves and should-haves and ask yourself, "If I had a life that looked like this, would I be overjoyed and fulfilled?" If the answer is no, ask yourself what's missing. Perhaps you need to rearrange something up from the would-be-nice bucket, or maybe something is missing altogether.

When you feel good about your prioritized list, consider running it by some friends and mentors to get their sense of how well it aligns with what they know about you. You want to go into the next step with as solid a list of priorities as you can.

Part 3: Visioning

With your fulfillment interests clear, you can update your Interests Profile, which will have changed, probably dramatically, during your growth and progress since you created it way back in Phase 1. The third part of this exercise asks, "What would a future that meets all of my highest priority interests look like?" As mentioned above, this image of the future is your Phase 4 vision. This is the target you are seeking throughout Phase 4. When you begin your conversations with connectors in Phase 4, you will start to pursue this vision by seeing what kinds of general feedback you get and figuring out what kind of team to create or join to achieve this vision. You'll then negotiate with Phase 4 decision makers to find collaborators who can join you in making your vision a reality. Throughout the process of Phase 4, your vision may change shape, but for now, creating a vision that clearly responds to your reformulated Interest Profile is the name of the game.

For starters, consider your must-have lists: How many of them have you starred? If not many are starred, you may realize that your current work and lifestyle are meeting your must-have interests quite well. If so, that's wonderful! You might need to make only minor shifts—if any—to lead a deeply fulfilling life.

It's important to note that we are not advocating that you make big changes in your life just for the sake of change. Your situation and your interests might change several years down the road, in which case you may feel the need to reevaluate and re-vision then, but for now you could be right where you need to be. However, if, like Justin, at the end of your appreciative inquiry and prioritization work you see holes where your current work setup is failing to meet your fulfillment interests, now is the right time to formulate your vision for a future in which those interests are met.

And now for the visioning work. On a new page, answer this question: "What would my life be like if all of my must-have interests were being met?"

Looking over your prioritized lists, a vision for the future may pop out at you. If so, great! Write it down. But, the perfect vision may not instantly spring to mind. That's also fine; try to draft a set of options. You are not committed to anything you write down, so allow yourself to jot down good, bad, and off-the-wall thoughts that come into your mind. Once you have a few ideas to work with, evaluate them against your must-have interests and select the one that best meets your fulfillment interests. If there are several that meet all your must-have interests, move on to your should-have interests. How about the nice-to-haves? Working through your interest priorities, you may find that one or two of your vision ideas—your options—are most compelling. In all likelihood, you will come back to your interest lists and vision ideas in the days and weeks following this exercise to modify them. Our re-visioning exercise is meant to kick off your Phase 4 process.

When Justin completed this exercise, he started with the big-picture vision and then let his thinking drift back toward more concrete steps he could test with connectors.

JUSTIN: My vision is to work for a business that serves companies and nonprofits using their work as a force for good. The dream is to have the majority of these be long-term client relationships where the client allows us to collaborate closely with their leadership team to ensure that we can tailor our services to be exactly what they need. I want to be working with clients committed to making effective communication and collaborative negotiation skills into institutional habits.

From a lifestyle perspective, the main shifts would be to have a job that is flexible enough to allow me to start a little later in the day so that I would have time to stretch and meditate before work and to leave space for me to have regular default social activities that bring me together with friends and new people in a consistent and low-effort way.

Thinking about what this would look like, practically, I could imagine one option to be joining an existing company in a role that involved course design and marketing focusing on companies using business as a force for good. A second option would be to build collaborations with other conflict management professionals interested in creating lasting behavior change to create new training methodologies and then apply that new intellectual property to developing my own work with environment- and social justice–oriented clients.

A final idea would be to work with foundations and venture capitalists to sponsor training and coaching for the organizations they fund or invest in. This way I could work with smaller organizations that need but cannot afford the kind of negotiation and communication support that I can offer. The relationship with larger institutions could allow for longer-term relationships and a focus on change and results. In each of these contexts, I would have to negotiate flexibility to meet the lifestyle interests on my must-have list.

In the short term, what I think this means is taking several months to explore which of these visions seems most promising to meet my must-have interests and meeting with connectors to see if there are other ways to get to my vision that I have not thought of.

Once you have a set of fulfillment priorities to work with and you've started to draft your vision, your final step before moving on to negotiating with connectors is to update your story to reflect this high-level self-negotiation.

Making Yours a Story of Fulfillment

Just like in the earlier phases, you'll want to distill your story down to its key elements in preparation for your meetings with connectors. The overall structure of your Phase 4 story is similar to previous phases, with some important differences. The "Passion" section of your story can now be replaced by a "Vision" section. This is your chance to share a snapshot of your Phase 4 vision with your connectors as a work in progress. And your call for support, or ask, will depend on how clear and achievable your vision already is. We'll discuss how to craft a helpful Phase 4 call for support in the next chapter. For now, your new story structure looks like this:

1. Biographical Information—details about you and your career progression to date that will (1) help the person you are meeting with connect with you and (2) give them a context

2. Vision—your new target

3. Interests—the basic motivations behind your vision, primarily based on the impact and lifestyle must-haves you identified

4. Constraints—places where you see conflicts between your impact and lifestyle interests that you don't know how to overcome

5. Call for Support—a request for advice—what they would do if they were in your shoes, with the specifics depending on how much you already understand about what your vision and must-haves entail

Next you'll be telling your story to enlist targeted support from connectors as you did in Phases 1 through 3. As you progress, you'll also share your story—in particular, your vision for fulfillment—with your peers and connectors in a way that spreads your plans and ambitions into their channels of knowledge and influence. You'll share your story with the hope that over time you'll ignite relationships of mutual support and interconnection with those who can amplify your vision as you support theirs.

11

Boosting Your Vision

Now that you have an articulated vision of fulfillment—or at least a list of your most important fulfillment interests—it's time to share this with your connectors. As in every other phase, you will approach people as connectors, with a targeted ask—this time, to build on the negotiation you just completed with yourself about your vision.

At the same time, you'll be reaching out to your peers for feedback and support. By now, some of your connectors have no doubt become peers, and vice versa. They know you, and you're comfortable bouncing ideas off of each other and entertaining half-baked theories. When you meet with peers, you may not have a formal or specific ask, and that's okay—you're just talking, which so often leads to unexpected insights. But their importance does not end there; your peer connections can significantly boost your Phase 4 progress in other ways. Through their networks, your peers can broadcast your vision out far beyond the horizon of your own contacts. Through those same networks, connectors may also funnel resources and potential collaborators back your way. The importance of surrounding yourself with inspiring peers is particularly key here in Phase 4 as you shoot for bigger dreams and pursue your most fulfilling lifestyle and impact interests.

This section takes up both of these contexts—targeted help

from connectors and more casual, free-form interactions with your peer community.

Having a strong set of peer connections is important for many reasons, not the least of which is that your peers can amplify your vision and connect you to resources that might not have otherwise come your way. Justin, for instance, is always involving peers in work ideas that excite him.

> *JUSTIN:* I talk about work all the time. I'm so passionately dedicated to what I do that I'm constantly scanning for people who can deepen my professional development or further one of the projects I'm working on. When someone mentions something they're doing that's relevant to what I'm working on, it catches my attention immediately and I try to learn more about their interests. I am on the lookout for ways we can connect professionally or spread the word about each other's projects.

For you and your peer connectors to get the most out of interacting, you have to connect regularly. This often requires being deliberate, particularly because your peers are very likely busy. Simply relying on bumping into them is a sure way *not* to see them. It can help to negotiate a system or routine for getting together as peers—and to ensure that your time together is engaging and productive, and also convenient. Of course, what this looks like will depend on the nature of your relationship and the interests and constraints in play.

Tad has a colleague—let's call her Bethany—who is accomplished, ambitious, and, as it turns out, very, very busy. Tad recognized that they were well suited to be peer connectors because they are both established professionals who operate within similar orbits, but have very different sets of experiences, know-how, and contacts to draw from. They both stood to gain a lot from being in regular contact and learning about each other's evolving visions. But they live in different states and have their own busy lives. How could they realistically keep in touch?

TAD: Because Bethany and I both often work on writing projects, a strategy we've used a couple of times for staying in touch professionally is partner-writing sessions, where we help push each other along, share ideas, and give one another feedback. When we're both in the middle of a writing project, we have a three- to five-hour writing buddy session online, where we start out discussing what we're working on, what we plan to accomplish in the next hour, and what we anticipate will get in the way. Every hour we check in about what we accomplished (or not) and what we plan to accomplish in the next hour. We also encourage one another.

This partnership makes writing—an important task for both of us in our professional development—easier and more fun. And each time we connect around writing, we also update each other on our broader career visions, progress, and stumbling points. From these updates, we end up being mindful of things that the other might find helpful. My interests, in other words, end up in play for Bethany, and vice versa. For instance, when Bethany was putting together a book about how to handle tricky conversations about money, she asked me to contribute a chapter about asking for a raise. When I had a client whose ideas were being dismissed by her team and superiors, I asked Bethany for ideas and a referral to someone who could be helpful.

These kinds of peer meet-ups provide an opportunity for each person to gain access to the other's networks of knowledge and contacts. By plugging your interests into your peers' networks—by consistently sharing your evolving story—you multiply the likelihood that others will pick up on or pass you things related to your vision. In the end, your vision ends up with more eyes and ears, and more legs. And the more people who are aware of your next-step ambitions, the more likely you are to have them come back to you later and say, "Hey, I saw something that's right up your alley." It can be an enormous help when peers act as each other's sounding boards and then spread ideas through their networks.

In a nutshell, you want to find ways to be in regular contact with peers so that you can plant and water the seeds of your vision. By putting your interests and plans out there, your vision can reach further. And this kind of deliberately fostered connection gives you the opportunity to support your peers in kind. Be their support and share in each other's enthusiasm.

What Makes Big Dreams Come True

As in previous phases, you will be reaching out to connectors beyond your peers in a targeted way. After all, you're probably still trying to figure out the best way to meet the fulfillment interests you identified in your re-visioning work. Your initial conversations with connectors in Phase 4 will be aimed at testing out and giving detail to your vision for fulfillment. With those details, connectors can help you (1) determine precisely what kinds of collaborations will advance this vision, (2) identify specific people with whom you might collaborate, and (3) anticipate what their interests might be. Your end goal in your Phase 4 negotiations with connectors is to figure out what sort of team you might need in order to realize your vision and move your working life to that next level of fulfillment. The team you either assemble or join (which we'll cover in the next chapter) can take many shapes depending on the nature of your vision. But first you need to ask for feedback from your connectors on your vision and how to rally others around that vision. Does it make sense to them, given your career profile and must-have interests? Do they see other clear alternatives? The scope of your ask depends on how clear your vision and next steps are *to you*.

A clear vision? If you're working on developing a clear vision, then peers, familiar connectors, and colleagues who know something about your evolving story will probably be able to give you the most helpful feedback. You may need more help prioritizing or making sense of your interests. One of the main reasons people get stuck at this point is that they need some help converting some of their more abstract interests into real-life actions plans.

- Ask: I want to work to support gender equity but I am not sure which of the many ways I could do this would fit me best. What do you think?

A team context for your vision? You know roughly what you want to achieve but can't see how to rally a team around the goal.

- Ask: I'd like to grow my small consulting firm and still have time to tour with my Bon Jovi cover band. What kind of team might make sense given this vision?
- Ask: How much of this can I do on my own, and where do I need support?

Knowledge of how to find teammates? You have a good sense of what kind of team you need, but you don't know where to find the members.

- Ask: I'm looking for accountants who specialize in microfinance, and I need at least two who speak Spanish and are willing to travel to Latin America. Where could I find these folks?
- Ask: I'm looking for a place where I can do both clinical mental health work and advocacy, and I want to be surrounded by people who are committed to reforming the criminal justice system. Do you know of any organizations that gather together around these core concerns and values?

Understanding the interests of potential team members? You have a clear vision, some viable options for a team, and you know who you want to be on that team, but you don't know how best to appeal to those potential collaborators.

- Ask: I'm interested in bringing Bryce on as a marketing assistant. Given what you know about him, what do you think I could offer him as a collaborator that would meet his interests and get him excited about joining us?

Ways to set up your team? You have good answers to the above questions, and you're ready to reach out and start negotiating with potential decision makers and collaborators, but you have practical questions about how to get set up.

- Ask: How and where would this team need to work? What kind of equipment or facilities needs should I be anticipating?

The answers to these questions—and any other wisdom your connectors happen to impart—will be vital for reaching out to potential collaborators in the next chapter. Even if you think that your target vision is crystal clear coming out of your re-visioning work, you may be surprised at how much it can benefit from the input of a wide range of connectors. Consider our friend Allison, a successful landscape architect who recently realized that her interests were leading her into the related field of landscape conservation.

Allison just wasn't getting certain things from her landscape architecture practice. She missed doing research, but above all, she craved the collaborative fieldwork and cultural exchanges that take place when many different people come together to work on large cultural heritage sites. Hence her initial Phase 4 vision: to be part of a multidisciplinary conservation team that preserves fascinating but threatened landscapes.

Allison's initial strategy was to join UNESCO, the United Nations Educational, Scientific and Cultural Organization, and so she reached out to connectors for their guidance on how she might land a role there. After meeting with several connectors—a gardens archaeologist, a cultural geographer, a producer at UNESCO, and several landscape conservationists—she found out that neither UNESCO nor any other single organization actually brought together the experts and the methods she thought were necessary to do the kind of conservation work she envisioned. At this point, she realized that she needed to step back and get a clearer sense of how to make her vision a reality.

She tapped into her network of connectors again, this time with a focus on what type of team she needed to do the kinds of projects she had in mind. With this change in ask, one of her connectors suggested she get in touch with two innovative conservation firms overseas that focused on the kind of cross-disciplinary work she found exciting. By negotiating short volunteer stints with both of these conservation firms, while staying at her current practice, Allison got a chance to observe who was doing cutting-edge work and where. She also got to be in a position to see that there were missing links and missed opportunities for coordination between landscape conservationists and architects. At this point, it occurred to her that she needed to create a team: a new kind of consulting firm that was going to seize these missed opportunities and bridge this gap.

Allison's asks evolved further. Now she had to figure out what kind of specialists she needed on her multidisciplinary team to land the big consulting projects she hoped for. And how would her firm be structured for legal and tax purposes? What kind of company, exactly, was she building? Here she had to reach out to people outside of her field—people who knew how to create an enterprise from scratch. The best advice she got came from a friend of a friend who had branched out of academic research several years before to start his own robotics company. He told her to get the team together and get the ball rolling: "You can figure out the broader business model later; for now, get the team together and get a project under your belt. Don't lose momentum trying to sort out too many details in advance. If the team works, you'll figure all that out."

On her connector's recommendation, Allison began reaching out to a list of potential team members—a geographer, an archaeologist, a conservationist, and two architects. Her vision ended up changing dramatically as a result of her conversations with connectors. Only a few months earlier, her plan was to join UNESCO; now she's building a unique consultancy. The former plan wasn't a bad one, but this new path more directly targets her must-have interests and is a stronger articulation of her vision.

And that is really the end goal of your conversations with connectors in Phase 4—producing the best version of your fulfillment interests that you can and a road map for going forward.

12

Going It Together

As you begin to develop a picture of your future team, you're at the brink of actualizing your Phase 4 vision. So far in Phase 4 you've negotiated with yourself to articulate a vision for meeting your enhanced impact and lifestyle interests. You've negotiated with Phase 4 connectors to clarify that vision and to brainstorm what type of team you'll need to actualize it. Now it's time to negotiate with Phase 4 decision makers. Who are the decision makers in Phase 4?

In earlier stages of your career, decision makers were often gatekeepers: the people who made decisions about whether to grant you access to jobs, internships, academic programs, and other opportunities. Now that you're more established in your chosen field, you're less dependent on other people to grant you access. You're already in, so you have more capacity to create your own opportunities. Phase 4 is about fine-tuning your work-life balance—and finding the right team to make that happen. Because of your advanced standing within your field, you might be in a decision maker role hiring other people. Alternatively, the decision makers you encounter in Phase 4 might be more like peers than superiors, in which case your negotiations are likely to be more collaborative than they were in previous phases. Because of this, we use the term "collaborator" in addition to "decision maker" in this chapter.

As you focus your energy on developing a specific opportunity that could fulfill your vision, keep exploring alternative ways to fulfill the vision too. It's essential to pursue multiple opportunities for fulfilling your vision. Having alternatives to consider gives you a much better footing in the negotiation itself, removes most or all of the anxiety about a particular opportunity not working out, and avoids having to start from square one if indeed it doesn't.

While negotiating with potential collaborators, explore whether there is a good fit between your interests and theirs. It's worthwhile being mindful of your standing relative to your potential team members. This will inevitably affect the tone of your initial fit conversations. In some cases, you'll be the primary decision maker. In others, you won't be a decision maker at all, even though you're realizing *your* vision. In general, there are three forms that your Phase 4 team-creation process can take.

1. *You are brought on by a decision maker.* When you decide that the classic setup of applying for a job and getting hired onto an existing team is the best way for you to meet your fulfillment interests, you will negotiate with the decision maker who is in charge of that team. This type of negotiation might look similar to your Phase 3 negotiations with decision makers, with the important difference that you'll be focusing on meeting your Phase 4 fulfillment interests.

2. *Teaming up with peers.* If your vision is shared by other decision makers, you might choose to unite your resources with theirs, as peers, where there is no clear hierarchy. In this scenario, instead of negotiating for a job, you are negotiating the terms of a collaborative partnership.

3. *You are the primary decision maker.* If you decide to build your own team, then you will be the primary decision maker hiring others.

Whether you decide to join an existing organization, team up with peers, or become a decision maker hiring others, it's important to explore your alternatives. Recall the importance of having alternative job offers in the "Alternatives Give You Power" section in chapter 9. Here in Phase 4, the context shifts: Your alternatives are now the various potential teammates you *could* bring on or the other existing teams you *could* join.

In your Phase 4 conversations with connectors, you scouted for potential collaborators. Now you'll focus more intentionally on fostering those relationships. Meeting with numerous potential teammates will give you a better sense of what your team could and should look like. The more you explore your alternatives—ways you could meet your interests other than the current collaboration you are exploring—the better informed you will be about what's out there. This, in turn, will give you more power as you negotiate to settle the terms and details of your eventual collaborations.

Exploring many alternatives up front can also be useful after you've formed your team, because unforeseen circumstances may require you to dip back into your pool of alternatives. There are many reasons why a well-conceived collaboration might not work out. If you've done a good job considering your alternatives up front, before you finally settle on a team arrangement, you are more likely to have access to good replacements if circumstances require you to change up the team down the road.

Bringing Collaborators into Your Vision

Coming out of your recent conversations with connectors, you have potential collaborators in mind. With any luck, you also have a sense of their interests. But how should you pursue them? Your goal is to negotiate a fit between your vision and their interests, but we suggest that you do this over the course of two separate conversations: an early fit negotiation and a later fit negotiation.

At various points in this book, we have offered advice on how to set up and conduct conversations with decision makers. By now interest-based negotiation conversations are probably second nature to you, so we won't retrace our steps too much. Here we just want to suggest a basic structure to get you thinking about how these fit conversations would ideally go.

The first step, the early fit conversation, is an exploratory conversation intended to allow you to share your vision, learn about the other person's vision, find possible overlap, and explore what a collaboration might look like in general terms. If you discover during this early fit meeting that your visions overlap and a collaboration seems promising, then you'll come back for a follow-up meeting—but only after you've both had time to step away and reflect on the first conversation.

During the later fit meeting, you and your potential team member will brainstorm concrete options for how collaboration could meet your fulfillment interests and theirs. If this conversation yields a promising set of options, you'll work out the details and make a commitment to team up.

Early Fit Negotiation

To prepare for your early fit conversations, make sure to take the time to (1) articulate to yourself your impact and lifestyle interests, (2) consider what interests might be most important to the potential collaborator you're about to talk to, and (3) sketch out some options for a setup that could satisfy both of you.

Remember how you prepared to negotiate a fit in Phase 3, which we addressed in chapter 9, "Rethinking the Interview and the Offer"? The same process applies here. For now, your main focus should be on interests and options. The key is to have the early fit conversation without committing to a project. To do this well, you will have to strike a balance between making clear that you are interested in potential collaboration and indicating that any collaboration is contingent on finding an option that meets your interests as well as your collaborator's interests. Here are the essential topics to consider in advance of each conversation.

1. Knowing your decision maker or collaborator: Who are you meeting with? Do your homework to make sure you know where they're coming from.

2. Framing and relationships: How can you send a strong collaborative signal in the beginning of the negotiation? What could you do to develop or improve the relationship? Are there low-risk, low-cost offers you can make to build trust, for example, in relation to status, respect, reputation, or appreciation? How will you:

   a. Start the conversation to check in about what is going on in their life and share some of what is happening in yours? What are some commonalities you can connect through?

   b. Frame the conversation as a joint exploration around fit?

   c. Appreciate them—their expertise, the quality of their previous work, their time, and so on?

3. Their interests: What might their needs, desires, motivations and fears be in this negotiation? Why might they be doing what they are doing or saying what they are saying?

4. Their vision, then yours: Ask about their vision before explaining yours. Questions you might ask to better assess their interests:

   a. Why do you do this work?

   b. What is your vision for yourself in five years?

   c. What does a healthy work-life balance look like for you?

   d. What is the impact you want to have on the world through your work?

   e. What else is important to you that would be good for me to know about?

5. Your interests: What are your needs, desires, motivations, and fears in this interview? Why are you making this particular ask?

6. Summarize your interests: Put into one sentence what you need to create a fit.

    a. My vision is . . .

    b. I see this collaboration contributing to the vision by . . .

    c. My initial thoughts are that the team will be made up of . . . doing . . .

    d. I'm interested in your perspective. What do you think? Do you have any additional ideas?

7. Next steps: Wrap up the conversation before making any final decisions, even if leaving the conversation without an agreement feels awkward.

    a. How will you express appreciation for their time and suggest taking time to think over what you have discussed?

    b. How will you schedule getting back together to discuss terms if you both continue to see a fit after stepping back?

Sample: "This has been really exciting. I think we've come up with several really good ideas here. I want to sleep on this and talk it over with one of my colleagues. I imagine that you want some time to ruminate as well. Let's get back together to think about if or how it makes sense to proceed after we've both had some time to reflect."

Once you have prepared for the conversation, consider setting an agenda. Although there are many ways to structure an early fit conversation, we suggest this simple breakdown, which we discuss in detail below.

1. Set a positive relationship tone.
2. Ask about their interests.
3. Share your vision.
4. Explore overlap.

1. Set a Positive Relationship Tone

Setting a collaborative tone from the start shows your potential teammate that you are committed to working *together* during this negotiation and in the future. Making this first overture to set a collaborative tone can powerfully shape your interaction and help your prospective teammate settle into conversation. After all, you've invited them to talk because you see the potential for mutual benefit. The tone of the negotiation is partly set by how you lead off. The default for many people is to hold their cards close to their chest when they don't know exactly what is being proposed. At the beginning of the conversation, they will be assessing whether it is safe to share their interests with you. By opening with a clear, collaborative message, you are making it more likely that they will share those interests with you, and that you will have a more transparent, productive negotiation.

A collaborative opening can be simple. It starts with a check-in, which can take different forms depending on your relationship going into the meeting. Even through a brief exchange about your weekend, upcoming plans to travel, favorite sports team, a work challenge, or funny anecdote, you establish a dynamic that encompasses more than just business. This kind of check-in increases the likelihood that the other person will connect with you on a personal level rather than just as a potential collaborator.

When Justin began negotiating with potential collaborators in Phase 4, he was looking for a team member who could help with writing negotiation simulation cases, researching articles, and editing this book you're currently reading. Through his connectors, Justin met a writer named Cara and asked her if she was willing to have a conversation to explore the possibility of working together on a set of research and writing projects. Below is an overview of how Justin opened the conversation with the following relationship gestures.

Checking in before getting down to business. Justin's invitation to check in conveyed that he saw Cara as a peer and that what was going on in her life interested him. Checking in allows you to connect as people, beyond the specific project you're discussing—which is not only enjoyable, but also an important test of collaboration chemistry.

Framing the conversation as a joint exploration around fit, rather than a one-sided evaluation. Justin made sure not to assume that Cara wanted the job, but rather that she would make a decision based on how well it met her interests. To convey this he said, "I'm really glad we're taking the time to meet today. If we do decide to work together, I want to make sure that it works well for both of us."

Appreciating something about them that reinforces why you reached out in the first place. This could be things like the quality of their previous work, their creativity, or how highly they were recommended. Make sure to thank them for taking the time to meet with you. Justin first referenced the writing samples Cara had provided, noting that her skill as a communicator was obvious. Then, he expressed his appreciation that she was willing to take the time to meet with him.

2. Ask About Their Interests

After your collaborative opening, try to learn more about the other person's work interests before expressing your own. Ask them to share in greater detail their own hopes or targets for the future.

When we present this approach to our coaching clients, many find it counterintuitive to inquire about the other person's interests before sharing their own. It's your team, so your vision should be up front and center, right? At some point, yes. In an early fit conversation, however, asking about their interests before explaining your own allows you to learn what is important to them for the future prior to discussing how your interests might align, without pointing them in a particular direction. Justin was considering bringing Cara onto his team. Before he introduced the type of writing he hoped she might do for him, he asked her about her relationship to writing and her writing-specific interests.

> *Justin:* "You mentioned that you were interested in writing. What kinds of things have you done, and what are you hoping to do in the future?"

Cara: "I've always gravitated towards writing essays and nonfiction. And now that I'm working in psychology, I'm having a lot of fun finding creative new ways to mesh my writing skills with this field."

With this, Justin could respond with follow-up questions. He learned what kinds of writing inspire Cara without directly influencing her answer.

Consider the alternative:

Justin: "I'm looking for someone to help me develop content for negotiation cases. Is that something that interests you?"

Cara—if she were just focused on getting a job: "Yes, absolutely."

In this second scenario, it would be hard for Justin to gauge if his and Cara's interests genuinely align.

3. Share Your Vision

Once you understand your potential collaborator's interests well enough—perhaps they've even shared with you something like a Phase 4 vision—share the story you developed during your Phase 4 negotiation with yourself to convey your vision and motivations.

In Justin and Cara's conversation, Justin shared that he wanted to improve the way people negotiate in the fields of environmental sustainability and social justice so that they could more successfully accomplish their missions. He shared his interest in keeping a sane pace of life and building community in Boston. He also shared his interest in developing as a thought leader around negotiation skills and behavior change, and he needed a writer to support him in clarifying his ideas, testing them, and then putting them down on paper.

4. Explore Overlap

Once your interests are laid out on the table, focus on the overlap. Justin and Cara identified a shared interest in incorporating social psychology research into writing projects. They brainstormed around this shared interest and identified three ways a collaboration could materialize: research projects to analyze data collected from Justin's previous negotiation students, starting a blog that explored how people actually change their negotiation behavior, and bringing Cara onto the editing team for this book.

Wrapping Up the Conversation (for Now)

When you reach a point in the conversation where you have sufficiently explored overlap in your interests, you should bring the conversation to a conclusion and step away to reflect. This moment of leaving the conversation without an agreement may feel a little awkward, but you need time to think over the discussion.

To transition out of his meeting with Cara in a way that left room for a second meeting, Justin ended his conversation with her by saying, "This has been great. I'm excited about the potential here, and I think we've come up with several good ideas. I want to sleep on this, and I imagine you do too. Let's get back together soon to think about how it makes sense to proceed."

After stepping away, use this time to evaluate the pros and cons of working with this person. Decide if you want to continue to explore the option of working with them. A solid commitment to working together can come only after you iron out what collaboration will look like, in detail, which is the work of the later fit conversation.

Later Fit Negotiation

If you decide to pursue a follow-up conversation, you'll need to update your prep notes to reflect what you learned during the early fit conversation, and to focus on objective standards and predictable surprises—again, similar to what you did in the "Negotiating the Offer" part of Phase 3 (chapter 9). Answering the questions about the topics below will help you prepare for the later fit conversation.

1. Overlap in visions: What interests of theirs emerged as most important during your early fit conversation? What interests of yours do you believe they could meet well based on your early fit conversation?

2. Options: What ideas do you have for options that would meet your shared interests? How could you make these ideas better? Be sure to include options that meet your impact and lifestyle interests, and theirs.

3. Objective standards: What seems fair to you? What existing criteria or standards can help you demonstrate that your request is fair and justified? Research how other people have put together similar collaborations or what organizational experts would advise.

4. Your alternatives: What other offers do you have? What will you do if you cannot come to an agreement with this decision maker? Which is your most attractive alternative?

5. Their alternatives: What will they do if they cannot come to an agreement with you?

6. Commitment: What form should your agreement take? Contracts, verbal agreements, and memorandums of understanding are just some of the options.

7. Predictable surprises: What might happen in the future that could cause problems between you? What language could you add to the agreement to anticipate and deal with these potential situations in advance? For instance:
   a. Does it make sense to do a trial period?
   b. Should your employment be linked to meeting targets? What happens if those targets aren't met?
   c. How will you divide up the spoils if the venture becomes wildly successful?
   d. If unexpected logistical challenges arise, who will be responsible for managing them?

8. How will you celebrate if you reach a mutually beneficial agreement?

For later fit conversations, we recommend the following structure, which we discuss in detail next.

1. Check in and review interests.
2. Talk about concrete options.
3. Decide if you want to work together.
4. Consider what could go wrong—or right.

1. Check In and Review Interests

As with the early fit conversation, be sure to take time at the beginning of the conversation to check in, appreciate your counterpart, and set an agenda for the conversation. Because some time has passed since your first conversation, it is helpful to recap and clarify the interests you talked about in the first meeting and share the relevant insights you gained from the reflecting you've both done since then.

2. Talk about Concrete Options

Think of this part of the conversation as being like arranging furniture in a room. The final arrangement you decide on represents the option you choose for your collaboration, and the furniture pieces represent different elements of the option that best meets your interests. The process of finding the best option is like adding, removing, and shifting the furniture around the room until you have it just the way you want it. This may take some time.

A key question to ask throughout the process of firming up options is: Is this arrangement fair to both of us? Fairness is critical, because if either person in a collaboration feels they are vulnerable to any degree of exploitation or being taken for granted, the work—not to mention the relationship—will eventually suffer. This is the time to engage with objective standards. How do your various ideas stack up against industry norms? Are there laws or well-accepted best practices that you could apply to your situation?

Once you think you've found the best arrangement, step back and look to see if there is an adjustment or two you could make that would improve the room even more for both of you. Maybe you want to move the couch a few inches to the left or add a new lamp, and your counterpart wants to get rid of the mirror. Ask yourselves: Do these changes make the room—the agreement—better for both of us? This is the time to consider these adjustments, even if they seem small, to help ensure that you don't leave with an agreement that is suboptimal.

The value of seeking this kind of adjustment now rather than later is twofold: It's much easier to add and move furniture around when both of you are there with your sleeves rolled up. Also, there may be easy ways to make the arrangement better for one or both of you at little or no cost to the other. Not taking the time to explore final adjustments may waste a perfectly good opportunity to add value to your joint efforts.

In the case of Justin and Cara, after they had come up with a few options that could work for both of them, Cara expressed interest in learning more about the negotiation teaching industry. They discovered that having Justin invite Cara to sit in on his local trainings would add value to the deal for her without costing him anything.

3. Decide If You Want to Work Together

Now the room looks great—the agreement is exactly how you both want it. It's time to decide if you are actually going to work together. Ask yourselves, "Is there an alternative to working with this person that will better meet my interests?" As in Phase 3, if the answer is yes, you have two choices. You can simply pursue that alternative, or you can go back to creating options with your current potential collaborator and work together to try to improve the layout of the room again, aiming to make it better than your alternative. If the answer is no—that is, there is no preferable alternative—then it's time to sort out the additional details of working together.

4. Consider What Could Go Wrong—or Right

Beyond the basic questions of start dates, compensation, responsibilities, and so on, you will want to discuss what could come up unexpectedly and disrupt your agreement. Even having generated many concrete options for working together, it is difficult to predict how collaborations will play out. Your collaboration will depend on many things, such as the response of the market, how personalities fit together within the team, performance or skill development of certain members, and many other factors outside of your immediate control. All of this uncertainty can be unnerving, but you can get a head start by anticipating how things might go. Just as in your Phase 3 negotiations, this is the time for you and your collaborator to discuss the predictable surprises that you brainstormed while preparing for this fit conversation.

Making Fit Last

When you have done your due diligence in negotiating with collaborators to ensure alignment of interests and vision, it takes much less effort to sustain fit and focus over time. Still, collaborative relationships will face challenges, despite your best efforts and intentions. People make three common mistakes in maintaining fit. The first is assuming nothing will change—believing that if your interests and visions were aligned at the outset, they will remain aligned. The second is falling out of a collaborative mindset when differences on the team emerge. The third is being unwilling to recognize when your interests are no longer aligned—something that's definitely hard to face when you've put so much into finding the right people for your team. Consider how all of these challenges emerged in the collaboration between Natalie and Wansuk.

Natalie is a woodworker who produces beautiful custom furniture. As her business grew, she brought on Wansuk to help her with business development, taxes, and administrative work—all things that kept her off the drafting table and shop floor where she wanted to be. Wansuk is a woodworking enthusiast who focused on entrepreneurship at business school. After being let go in a downsizing, he received a generous severance package that allowed him to work with Natalie for free for a few months as a trial. Natalie was pleased with his work and hired Wansuk after the trial. Natalie's vision, as she told Wansuk, was to make high-end furniture for clients who wanted their pieces to be functional and artistic. Wansuk was excited about the enterprise and the opportunity to work with Natalie, and Natalie was grateful to be able to focus on her craft and leave the business development to Wansuk.

Their collaboration grew the business substantially at first, but after a year, Natalie started to get orders that specified unusual types and sources of wood. One client requested recycled maple or oak from shipping pallets. The first few times this happened she complied, intrigued by the challenge. Upon receiving further similar requests, she asked Wansuk if he knew why this was happening. He told her he was exploring the market for people interested in renewable materials and probably some of those people had placed orders. Natalie stayed focused on the onslaught of orders that kept rolling in, but over time her clients got pickier about the wood they wanted, and she became more and more frustrated. She also noticed that fewer and fewer of her clients were high-end hotels and furniture stores.

After complaining several times to Wansuk about how much time she was wasting on these picky clients, Natalie realized that he still wasn't seeing the problem she saw. So she had a more direct conversation with Wansuk. She insisted that he shift his focus back to the types of clients they had started with—no more of these specialty requests for recycled wood. Wansuk responded by pointing out that he was responsible for the majority of the company's sales and that he was not willing to shift the business. If she wanted different clients, she could go out and do the marketing herself.

Exasperated, Natalie did not know what to do. After their conversation, she returned to the shop confused and frustrated. She considered raising the issue again but eventually decided she didn't want to risk stifling the momentum they did have, so she just focused on drafting and fabricating whatever orders came in.

Natalie and Wansuk didn't speak again about the direction of the business; they stopped spending time together as friends and said as little to each other as possible.

Natalie and Wansuk fell victim to some understandable—but avoidable—dynamics that can easily arise between team members. In the following sections we discuss three strategies for dealing with the three common problems that Natalie and Wansuk encountered during their collaboration.

Assume That Some Things Will Change

Natalie assumed that the well-aligned visions she and Wansuk had at the start of their collaboration would continue indefinitely. As her collaboration with him progressed and shifted, it would have been beneficial to check in and recalibrate the fit. The first obvious opportunity to do this was when she approached him about the renewable orders and realized that he had been seeking out a different client base. This interaction hinted at diverging interests and would have served as a good moment for Natalie to sit down with Wansuk and compare notes on where they saw the company heading.

If you notice that your team's work is no longer moving in the direction of your vision, this may imply that your vision and their interests have diverged, and it should cue you to ask yourself what happened: Have their interests changed? Have mine? Simply checking in about interests may be enough to get your collaboration back on track. In other cases, their interests, or yours, have shifted and you need to see what adjustments are needed to ensure a fit. If the gap between your visions is profound, explore whether it is worth continuing. Without a deliberate conversation about what is currently driving everyone's decision-making, it will be difficult to determine the causes and degree of misalignment.

Note that there is no need to wait until you notice misalignment; you can preemptively make alignment check-ins part of your periodic performance reviews, for instance.

Stay in a Collaborative Mindset

Although Natalie was cordial in her interactions with Wansuk, she defaulted back to being positional—insisting that he drop the renewables market. She failed to engage him in a conversation about their overlapping interests, which prevented them from exploring creative options for resolution. As coaches to organizations, we often see people fall into this pattern of positional behavior when differences arise. When things are going well, they have no trouble negotiating collaboratively. When things get challenging, though, it's easy to unintentionally slip into making demands, which leads people to act competitively or accommodate the other side to avoid the conflict, or ignore it altogether.

Rather than slipping into positional thinking—"it's either my way or your way"—it's possible to prioritize both the outcome you want and the strong relationship you want moving forward. You can accomplish this by focusing on the interests behind your respective positions. By this point in the book, focusing on interests is intimately familiar to you, so it will be no surprise that returning to them is what to do when you find yourself working at cross-purposes with your team. If you catch yourself or others getting positional, the best way to shift away from positional behavior is to ask the question "Why?" This question gets at what's *behind* the positions. You may want to ask variants like "Tell me more," "Why is that important to you?" or "What would you get out of that?" The approach is always the same: attend to the underlying interests rather than engaging the positions.

Natalie could have reestablished a collaborative conversation when she noticed that she and Wansuk were getting positional by making this shift from positions to interests. Only then would they be able to brainstorm ways to move forward as partners, doing work that inspires them while maintaining a positive working relationship. A collaborative conversation between them might sound like this.

Natalie [stating position]: It seems like you just want to build furniture for customers that like renewable materials. That won't work for me!

Wansuk [stating position]: And all you want is to build fancy furniture that is basically artwork for hotels and the furniture stores downtown. I'm the one bringing in the clients. If you want to go out and get high-end clients, knock yourself out. But otherwise you're going to have to accept the work I bring in.

Natalie [moving to interests]: Clearly something isn't working here. You're right about who my ideal client is, but that's not all that's important to me. I want to create art, and I want to get challenging work that pushes me and makes me grow as an artist. The 'fancy hotels' are important to me because I like the hospitality world—it keeps me in tune with the luxury market and lets me network with people in that world. I also don't want to deal with administrative burdens. I'm tired of spending so much time on the website and marketing, and balancing the books on Friday nights. I want us to have a better relationship, and I want to have time to do my hobbies outside of work. [Inquiring about Wansuk's interests:] Help me understand what it is about the renewables market that is so attractive to you. What do you want from this partnership?

Wansuk [moving to interests]: You don't think I want the same things as you? Renewable materials are important to me, and I like to support local businesses, raise awareness about where materials come from, and promote a culture of recycled materials. But there are a lot of other things I care about. I didn't know you were balancing the books on Friday nights. I've been working like crazy too. I want a low-pressure job and I don't want to work 80-hour weeks. And who doesn't want to work with colleagues they enjoy? I also want to work with people whose artistic talents I admire.

Natalie [moving to discussing options]: Okay, looks like we
have a lot to talk about then. And we aren't saying entirely
different things here. Let's just look at where we agree for
now, and what is important to both of us. What ideas can
we think of for the business?

With the information they now have about their interests, Natalie and Wansuk would be able to brainstorm and come up with a
number of ideas and then use the list to generate even better ideas
before whittling it down to the best ones to pursue together. Some
of these could be:

- Explore furniture for high-end restaurants specializing
  in sustainable locally sourced food (who would likely care
  about where the wood comes from).
- Build a relationship with local foresters who can provide
  new cut, but renewably harvested, wood of the kind
  Natalie needs.
- Pitch luxury hotels on using recycled materials.
- Create a new service providing interior design consulting
  for hotels, which would not necessarily include building
  the furniture.
- Out of company profits, Natalie's salary, Wansuk's salary,
  or some combination, hire a marketing person to focus
  exclusively on the high-end furniture space, allowing
  Wansuk to continue his focus on recycled materials.
- Take a trip together into the world of sustainable
  materials for Natalie to learn more about Wansuk's
  passion.

That's not a bad list to work from!

Even though a collaborative approach to negotiation is the one
most likely to get both people what they want and preserve the relationship, when people are under pressure or triggered emotionally,
it can still be easy to slip into being positional at first. To maintain
a collaborative atmosphere, you will need to be alert to moments
when you or others on your team are starting to state what you want

in the form of inflexible demands. When that happens, step back and ask, "Why are we demanding what we're demanding?" Get at the interests behind the positions.

Be Willing to Reorganize the Team

When team members' visions do fall completely out of alignment, we often see people preserve teams as they are when that is not their best option. When a collaboration has run its course, there is no need for it to end in outright hostility. When Natalie first noticed the growing incongruence her motives and Wansuk's, she could have addressed it. Collaborating could have brought out their interests, inspired creative options, and saved a harmonious work-ing relationship. It's also possible that it could have shown them that their interests were incompatible moving forward and that their visions had become different enough that their best option was to dissolve their team.

If you' find yourself in a situation where you think you might need to dissolve a team, you should still frame the conversation around interests. Start by making sure you have considered whether continuing the team is worthwhile. (See "Assume That Some Things Will Change" on page 256.) If you surface major differences in your interests during that process, then it's time to raise the question of whether it makes sense to continue and, if so, how. You might start the conversation by saying something like this:

> *Example:* I can see that our priorities have shifted over the last several months and we are both increasingly frustrated with how things are going with the team. Would you be open to taking some time to revisit what's important to each of us and talk about what would need to change in order to remedy this situation for both of us? I bet that if we put our heads together we can come up with ways to work better as a team. I also wonder if we'll better meet our interests by parting ways. I guess the answer to that question will really depend on how our problem-solving goes.

Being aware of these three potential pitfalls that can damage collaborations will keep you focused on preventing them. Making sure interests are at the forefront throughout your collaboration will grant you the agility to support strong working relationships.

Your Next Destination

If this book has helped you to get a job that loves you back, then we are ecstatic! You reached this point because you took the time to get clear on where you wanted to go, worked to gain access to a new world, and negotiated for the right kind of opportunities, time and again. So what now?

Whether you reach Phase 4, Building Greater Fulfillment, at age 30, 40, or 70, you will find that what you need and want continues to shift. It would be unrealistic to imagine that your interests will not change going forward, or that you no longer need to concern yourself with the negotiation skills that got you this far. We laid out the four phases of this book as a simple linear progression because we believe that is the best way to learn them. In practice, you will likely discover that the thresholds between phases become murky. You may cycle through some of the phases a few times in a few different industries throughout your career as your interests and priorities shift. The good news is that no matter where you find yourself, the best tools for thriving throughout transitions in the future are the same three conversations you practiced throughout this book: negotiating with yourself about what you want, negotiating with connectors about how to get there, and negotiating with decision makers to make it happen.

At this point, the makeup and flow of these three conversations is hopefully second nature to you. You probably find yourself taking time to consider your interests before forging ahead with any given project or collaboration. When you come across new challenges, you are likely to seek out the wisdom of connectors who have been in your situation before. And, when the time comes to negotiate for what you want, you are more likely to figure out who the decision makers are and speak to them in a way that aligns interests and prioritizes fit.

When you started reading this book, you were probably hoping to get a job or escape an unfulfilling career. These three conversations helped you do that. And if you internalized them, as we have seen many of our coaching clients do, then you will find yourself using them far beyond career development. Understanding the world in terms of negotiations with yourself, with connectors, and with decision makers becomes a general approach to building projects and relationships.

For example, at work you might be tasked with creating a marketing campaign for a new product. This single assignment is not really a career development task, but you would still do well to start by checking in with yourself (and your supervisor) to figure out the key interests you are seeking to meet through the campaign. When you're clear on what's important to you, the next logical step would be to talk with people who know about marketing and, in particular, about the product you are working on. You would have conversations in-house with the marketing veterans. You would talk with some target customers. You might talk to your marketing consultant friend. To all of them, you would put forward your interests and ask, "If you were me, what would you do?" From these conversations you would be able to target specific key decision makers, like advertising sales reps. You will have a fit conversation about how well their media reaches your target market. In your conversations you will explore creative ways of working together. Then, based on other media vehicles available to you—your alternatives— you will either make an agreement to work together or move on.

An example of using this approach that's even further from professional ambitions is that of a young couple we coached who used it to buy a house in the greater Boston area, a notoriously competitive and complicated market, full of unwritten rules and conventions—a terrain rife with misapprehensions and missteps. They, too, started negotiating with themselves to determine their interests and constraints and then developed their story as home buyers. They built a network of connectors and collaborators to dramatically improve their understanding of the available housing stock, inspection processes, financing options, offer letters, seller interests beyond money, and so on. They managed to build a robust network of contacts and information and to clinch a sale on an ideal home in a matter of weeks, rather than months. A key element that influenced the seller who accepted their bid was an offer letter they wrote telling their story and addressing the seller's interests. Without their network, they would not have known how to frame their offer letter or what the seller's interests were.

As our three conversations begin to permeate the way you think about all interactions—not just career negotiations—you'll become increasingly more interest oriented. Instead of focusing on people's opening arguments, demands, or excuses, you will be adept at probing the interests hiding in the background; it will be second nature to you. Being interest oriented gives you the capacity to bring a different perspective and approach to making decisions, resolving disputes, building community, and getting ideas off the ground.

As you continue to use interest-oriented thinking throughout your career and life, you also have an opportunity to share it. When people seek you out as a connector, make time to meet with them, help them with their approach, and provide the information they seek. The success you've had in your career was aided by your ability to meet your connectors' interests but also by their good-hearted generosity. The best appreciation you can give to those connectors who helped you along is to create a welcoming career space for those who are now where you were. Assist people in need of support and counsel; help them learn not just about a particular field but also about how to negotiate, think in an interest-oriented way, and navigate career development as a phased process. Show them how generative a discussion with a connector can be—so many options! Explain the power of a yesable proposal and why it can be so welcome and successful. Help them focus on a fit conversation instead of an audition.

You now have a lot to offer as an interest-based negotiator, career developer, and team builder. Empower others with these skills and perspectives. Helping others find fulfillment in their working lives was our primary inspiration for writing this book, so we hope you will pass on the tools and wisdom that most inspired you!

Acknowledgments

Making the effort to thank people for their support
is essential, and here we have another opportunity
to practice what we preach.

Finding a Job That Loves You Back is the culmination of much trial and error, countless informational interviews, coaching sessions, professional ties, and conversations, and a strong desire to gather it all up and share it with a wider audience. This book has been several years in the making, and throughout the entire process we've benefited from many kinds of support—brainstorming, financial backing, reviewing, guiding, critiquing, and encouraging—from many people.

JUSTIN: I want to thank my whole family for modeling what living a life of meaning looks like. Thanks to my mother, Paula, for her tireless research support and constant flow of good ideas about how to bring the concepts in this book to a broader audience; my father, Alan, for his consistent encouragement and providing me with many opportunities to negotiate as a child; my sister, Nora, for her brilliant coaching insights; and my granddad, Oliver, for creating our first awesome working logo. A big thanks to the Habitus team's work on this! Nupur Amin, Lizy Freudmann, Radha Prabakaran, Kelsa Summer Roidt, and Dr. Kathy Gonzales, your work and support getting this book to the finish line has been invaluable! Last but not least, appreciation to Moni for seeing the value in the book and putting its advice to use immediately in your life.

CARLY: Thank you to all the wonderful people who kept believing in this project even though it took us ages to finish it! Your thoughts, support, feedback, and patience made this project possible. Thanks to all of you for being there in all the ways that you have been.

TAD: I thank my wife, Betsy, for her unconditional enthusiasm and support. My children, Will and Annie, added their thoughts, feedback, and motivation. My sisters and their husbands kept encouraging me not to give up on finishing the book: Cathey, Debby, Dennis, Cynthia, and Dan. My nephews offered continuous interest, referrals to connectors, and advice on crowdfunding, social media, and marketing. My cousins, stepfamilies, and in-laws shared their curiosity and excitement. Thanks to Ron for helping me make hard decisions about when to work on the book and when to focus on my career coaching. In addition, I so appreciate the people who worked together with me to reevaluate my career and what was important to me so that I could make my transformation into a book author: Geoff, Sarah, Zach, Kelly, Keith, Todd, Steve, Yolanda, Danielle, Judith, Gbeke, Ana Vera, Alan, the Michelles, and Roger.

Thanks Are Due to Many Others

To the people who trained, mentored, and inspired us about the world of negotiation and alternative dispute resolution at Program on Negotiation and MWI, including David Laws, Gillien Todd, David Seibel, Stevenson Carlebach, Bob Bordone, Debbie Goldstein, Doug Stone, Sheila Heen, Elaine Lin, Rachel Viscomi, Bruce Patton, Chuck Doran, Josh Hoch, Moshe Cohen, Diane Levin, Alan Price, Ericka Gray, Arline Kardasis, Crystal Thorpe, Vicky Bennet, Robin DiGiammarino, and Nnena Odim. And those who we have worked and collaborated with, including Allison McBratney, Lesley Foster, Marcus Stergio, Lisette Smith, Stephen Frenkel,

Nancy Connelly, Vicky Peterson, Kim Whelan, Mike Wheeler, Heidi Werther, Javier Calderon, Dan Green, Pete Dignan, Luis Gracia-Mon Martinez, Geraldine Bethencourt, and Jacobo Ducay Ferré. And a special mention to Blair Trippe, who not only introduced Tad to the ADR world, but also followed up with him to make sure he'd sign up for the basic mediation training!

To those at the Consensus Building Institute who spurred us on when the framework was barely a germ of an idea, including Larry Susskind, David Fairman, Pat Field, Merrick Hoben, Carri Hulet, David Plumb, Betsy Fierman, Stacie Nicole Smith, Mil Niepold, Ona Ferguson, Tushar Kansal, Eric Roberts, and Sossi Aroyan.

To the people who provided general knowledge, tips, insights, and ideas: Hal Movius for his feedback on our initial pitch and idea; Deborah Grayson Riegel for information about publishing; Steve Seeche for his reality testing and queries; Jodi Scheier for helping Tad find the inspiration to join the writing team; Tina Quick for encouragement and advice on self-publishing; Anne Copeland for supporting the project in its infancy; Sheila Puffer for advice on writing and potential publishers; and the whole Families in Global Transition Boston Affiliate group. Rachel Rybaczuk for being a wonderful professor and friend who equipped Carly with new ways to think and write about social class. We would also like to thank our preliminary coaching clients for giving us your trust and feedback. Debbie Goldstein, who not only taught the course at the Program on Negotiation with Gillien Todd that was both Justin and Carly's introduction to negotiation theory, but also generously mentored Justin through his first year in the world of conflict resolution. Justin attributes much of his success to the wisdom Debbie imparted to him in those coaching meetings early in his career. Without Debbie, Justin might not have made it into the field and many of the ideas in this book would never have occurred to us.

To those who worked on the nuts and bolts of the project: We would like to give special thanks to Lesley Foster, who kept us on task, found the wheels when they fell off, and made sure everything got done that had to be done. We would also like to thank Laura

Sánchez Garcia for her tremendous help on revamping our marketing; Allison Webster for redesigning our website; Ryan Bradley for providing preliminary copyediting support; and Siena Falino for producing our inaugural website, directing the communication to our backers, and researching the career book market.

For our RocketHub crowdfunding video, we would like to thank the D'Amore-McKim School of Business at Northeastern University, and specifically Professors Ed Wertheim, Brendan Bannister, and David Boyd for your support of our project and space for filming the video. And to Pam Weir, a warm thank-you for working your magic when we thought we were out of options. We also have to thank our videographers: Josh Meisel for his patience and perseverance through our first shoot and Scott Keenan for his direction and professional production throughout the process of our second shoot. And the video would not have had its character or flair if it were not for our artist and dear friend, Wes Nutter, who donated his time to both video shoots. Thank you to Michael Graskemper for helping us find space for our first shoot.

At various times during the writing, Tom Gorman was kind enough to provide his advice, as well as review some of our writing and give his feedback. That led us to creating a publishing team including developmental editor Lucas Freeman, who was the hub of the operation for so much of the project, and editor and publisher Ann Delgehausen at Vaerden & Co., who pushed us across the finish line. We'd like to thank the additional editors Cara Bigony and Dara Syrkin.

And lastly, we want to give an enormous thank-you to the backers of our RocketHub crowdfunding campaign, who gave us the financial support to pay the expenses of the project. We will always appreciate your confidence in us.

Our Crowdfunding Backers

Craig Altemose, Keith & Beth Armstrong, Judy Asselin, Becca Backer, Todd Barber, Yolanda Beech, Chris Bell, Cynthia and Dan Benfield, Cara Bigony, Matt Boole,

William Bradley, JJ Briones, Margaret Brown, Eshu Bumpus, Caroline Canning, Rob & Anne Carey, Tim Carey, Richard Carpenter, Gary Chan, Danielle Cleary, Heather Conrad, Aaron Cross, Garry and Anne Crowell, Nina Czeko, David and Judy Danielsen, Stacey and Bruce Danziger, Rob and Sarah DeFreitas, Jacobo Ducay Ferré, Miguel Escamilla, Siena Falino, Andrew and Carole Fargason, Lucas Freeman, Geoff and Sarah Gardner, Kevin and Dana Glynn, Samuel Gottstein, Henry and Joan Graber, Cara Graver, Kelly Gushue, Dan Hackney, Beth Hartin, Dave and Kate Haviland, Josh and Rachel Hoch, James and Hemsley Hughes, Carri Hulet, James Hwang, Andrew Inkpen and Patricia Seary, Anne Inkpen, David Inkpen, Terri James, Charo Juan, Jonna Kangasoja, Tushar Kansal, "Keenan" Keenan, Carson Keller, Berry Kennedy, Cathey Kennedy, Reed Kennedy, Scott and Anika Kessler, Paula Kline, Andrew Kraus, Peter Lane, Nancy Lesh, Diane Levin, Elly Lindsay, Ninetta Manousi, Joe and Barbara Marchese, Betsy Mayer, Frank Mazzola and Cindy Peterson, Kathy McLaughlin, Adam Mintz, Marney Morrison, Jamie Mosteller, Steve and Beth Murray, Stephanie Ngo, Bill Nutter, Wes Nutter, Debby and Dennis O'Brien, German Ortiz, Ray Pagliaro, Allie Perry, Charlie Pillsbury, Jay Pressman, John Pyne, Anne Rath, Andrew Ravenna, Mateo Reyes, Dan Roberts, Will and Heather Rodiger, Daniel Rossman, Rich and Hanne Rubin, Carolyn Ryffel, Alina Sapozhnikova, Jody Scheier, Ruth Scodel, David Seibel, Charlotte Seid, Paul and Heidi Slye, Joanna Snyder, Lesley Spencer and Max Foster, Becca Staples-Moore, Marcus Stergio, Anne Warner, Pamela Weir, Stephen and Susan Weiss, Ed Wertheim, Kim Whelan, William Whitaker, John White, Mary Wilder, Alex Wright, Toni Wu, Nathan Yi, Elizabeth Youngblood, Enzo Zamora D'Alessandro, Molly Zhitnik, and Alex, Becca, and Charlotte.

CPSIA information can be obtained
at www.ICGtesting.com
Printed in the USA
BVHW042147290323
661431BV00004B/114